The Reality of Life

Paul M. Nkofo

WESTBOW®
PRESS
A DIVISION OF THOMAS NELSON
& ZONDERVAN

Scripture taken from the Holy Bible, NEW INTERNATIONAL VERSION®. Copyright © 1973, 1978, 1984 by Biblica, Inc. All rights reserved worldwide. Used by permission. NEW INTERNATIONAL VERSION® and NIV® are registered trademarks of Biblica, Inc. Use of either trademark for the offering of goods or services requires the prior written consent of Biblica US, Inc.

Good News Translation® (Today's English Version, Second Edition) Copyright © 1992 American Bible Society. All rights reserved.

WestBow Press books may be ordered through booksellers or by contacting:

WestBow Press
A Division of Thomas Nelson & Zondervan
1663 Liberty Drive
Bloomington, IN 47403
www.westbowpress.com
1 (866) 928-1240

Because of the dynamic nature of the Internet, any web addresses or links contained in this book may have changed since publication and may no longer be valid. The views expressed in this work are solely those of the author and do not necessarily reflect the views of the publisher, and the publisher hereby disclaims any responsibility for them.

Any people depicted in stock imagery provided by Thinkstock are models, and such images are being used for illustrative purposes only. Certain stock imagery © Thinkstock.

ISBN: 978-1-4908-7246-9 (sc)
ISBN: 978-1-4908-7247-6 (hc)
ISBN: 978-1-4908-7245-2 (e)

Library of Congress Control Number: 2015903628

Print information available on the last page.

WestBow Press rev. date: 3/12/2015

Contents

To the girls: you are a God-given blessing in my life. You make me look forward to each day with hope. You are the blossoms that garnish my heart's hinterland without aid from the ever changing seasons and climate that define the exterior of the earth.

Tabitha 'Mathabo Nkofo & Beatrice Mantšanana Matsoso

Your portrait is forever carved on the walls of our subconscious minds, where it never gathers dust. We shall ponder your memories to our dusty demise!

Emma 'Matafita Nkofo, Magdalena Nomsa Nkofo, and Elizabeth Itumeleng Nkofo; as we daily drudge through the journey of life, you are an oasis of cool spring water to quench my thirst. You have become the gauze bandages and underlying cotton wool to retain blood from my gashes. You are a soothing daily ointment to calm the pain of my sores. But most of all, you are my friends and life companions!

Acknowledgements

Beginning when I was in secondary school, I developed the vision of one day publishing books. I have always wanted to live on in published media long after my flesh has retired. In June 2010 I started this humble project. My dream was to reach out to the world with a message that might be of great help to my fellow human beings. It is not feasible to travel to every corner of the globe, since the logistics would be cumbersome even if one had the funds. I then decided that the easiest way to answer the call and convey this message of humility to the entire world would be through writing a book. It is easier to disseminate a written communication throughout the world, especially with the Internet. I hope that in the future this publication will be translated into the different languages of the world.

I would like to thank the following people and organisations for making this dream a reality: Glory be to God the Father, the Son, and the Holy Spirit through His prophets: Father Peter John Masango and Mother Anna Seipati Masango, and Father Paul Thabang Matsoso and Mother Beatrice 'Malimakatso Matsoso. You have pulled me out of the prison of sin and continuously mould me into a better person.

A man and woman lived in abject poverty in the rural village of Ha 'Matafita in Matebeng (Christina 'Maphali Nkofo and Livingston Lira Nkofo). You brought me into this world and raised me up into the man I am today. Dad, from you I have learned the lessons of manhood in the countryside. Mom (may your soul rest in peace), you nested me on your back and fed me your breast. Oftentimes I did wet your back.

My wife and children (Emma Madavid, Magdalena Nomsa, and Elizabeth Itumeleng Nkofo), you have supported me throughout the challenging times and have made it possible for me to write this document, as I stole a lot of your time. Mr. Arthur Lelosa and Mr. Koali George Motlomelo, you gladly financed publication of this document when days were dark. Mr. Bheka Shezi, and Mr Thembela Mzolo, your support was invaluable. George Koali Motlomelo and Khotso Kobisi, I thank you for your editorial effort. I would also like to thank WestBow Press for their editorial work and agreement to publish this book.

Credit also goes to the Good News Bible Today's English Version (TEV) third edition, and Holy Bible New International Version (NIV) second edition. All biblical quotations in chapters have been taken from the Good News Bible (TEV), and the Holy Bible (NIV). Other references have been taken from the latest electronic version of Encyclopaedia Britannica (2014) and from the Book of Adam and Book of the Cave fromsacret texts.

I have walked precipitous slopes and been through numerous mountain passes. I have crossed various springs and raging rivers. I have walked across meadows, bush, scrublands, and barren deserts. I have dragged though stormy winds and cruised through gentle breezes. My feet have been swathed in the chilly snows and seared in the blazing sun. I have had my shoulder patted and my head banged. I am born out of an assortment of environmental circumstances. Simply, I am a chiselled herd boy.

Introduction

What is real and what is not? Is it the perception of our minds? What goes on in a madman's mind? He sleeps on the streets and rarely freezes to death. He traverses nature reserves full of animals perceived as dangerous and comes out without a scratch. He devours food out of dustbins and yet day by day continues to roam the streets on barefoot. He surely sees the rest of us as mad who consider ourselves "normal". The secret is embedded in the benthos of his subconscious mind. I hope that this simple writing, *The Reality of Life*, may challenge our minds and give us inspiration in our daily encounters in life.

The infinite river runs from a non-depleting constant spring in the future. The contents, bitter and sweet, are displayed on the ever expectantly lush banks of our present. The ocean of the past never overflows. It continuously shuffles its waters and splashes our shores to scatter and lay bare actions associated with the times of yore. The present is limited in duration but forever blithely dances in the confines flanked by the future and the past.

A thin gentle zephyr blows from an unidentifiable origin. It brushes past leaving fine dust sieve-trapped by our raiment. We feel the might but do not behold the form. The evident movement of vegetation indicates its direction. The aggregate of sand pebbles record footage of the otherwise intangible. Inconspicuously mounds of silt deposit shall form. Old trails steadily fade away with the imprint of new ones.

A waterfall leaps over a jetty edge beyond which our eyes do not see. Beneath, the patience of the flow has artistically worn hard rock into a bowl. Riparian vegetation opportunistically benefits from the tiny droplets that form into mist. The fog split opens the rays of the descending afternoon sun to exhibit an assortment of beautiful colours. Shortly the horizon embraces the sun, engulfing the landscape in darkness.

An incessant war is ever raging between the seasons that eternally gnaw upon each other from head to tail. The vestige of a season ascends to the next, transforming the land. The lilies and orchids that embroider our meadows, where tiny birds hop from flower to flower singing as they naively cross-pollinate, will soon go dormant. The marshlands will momentarily quiet down into muddy puddles.

An innocent grassland pipit leaves the warmth of her nest at the crack of dawn. She flaps her wings in merriment as she glides through and hugs the cool morning breeze. With the warmth of the rising sun, her hope for the morrow never ebbs. At midday a sun-scorched shepherd watches in mordant amusement as she displays her aeronautical skills. At dusk she dangles dead, hanging from the safety pin of his dirt-clogged blanket next to his bosom.

At nightfall her procreant cradle is exposed to chilly air. Her chicks wait endlessly for her warmth and an overdue meal. Their faint cry grows into a frantic call, spurred by gradually rising pangs of starvation and grief. Their destiny is left to resilience against the harsh elements presented by their hinterland, as their mother roasts on the flickering twilight inferno to satisfy human appetites.

What is time? The dictionary in *Encyclopaedia Britannica* defines time as "**a**: the measured or measurable period during which an action, process, or condition exists or continues: duration; **b**: a non-spatial continuum that is measured in terms of events which succeed one another from past through present to future." From this definition, it is clear that time is defined in relation to events. Hence, time may be referred to as a measure of events.

In time, we always refer to the past, the present, and the future, and the time measures used by different people vary, depending on their interests. For example, geologists and palaeontologists talk about billions, millions, and thousands of years. However, in our daily calendars we talk of millennia, centuries, decades, and years. On the other hand, those who work on experiments apply smaller units of time such as hours, minutes, seconds, and milliseconds.

Time has neither beginning nor end. That is, if one were to measure time into the past in mathematical terms, this would be infinity. The measurement of time to the future would also result in perpetuity. Since in our daily language we talk in terms of the past, the future, and the present, what and how much is the present? We can define the present as the time between the past and the future.

For argument's sake, let us consider the following diagram:

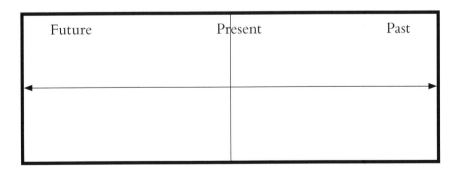

Fig. 1

If the thin line dividing the double headed arrow line represents where the future is becoming the past, the present is a very small amount of time indeed. In mathematical relationship, it can be said that the limit as time approaches the past is equal to infinity. It also follows that the same is true for the future. However, the limit as time approaches the present seems to be equal to zero (0). If this argument is true, the present can be defined as the point where the future is quickly becoming the past. It is clear therefore that even now as I speak, all that I say is quickly becoming the past.

From the diagrammatic representation above, in terms of measurement, the future clearly equals the past in magnitude. However, the difference is that the events of the past are known from a certain vantage point in time, but we do not know for certain what lies in the future. Since we can only live in the present, we are living in a point in time where the future is swiftly transformed into the past, and we do not know how much time from the future an individual will spend in present form.

However, when it comes to prophecies, it is absolutely phenomenal that, for example, Isaiah accurately spoke of the Messiah more than four centuries before He was born. How could this happen? Two possibilities come to mind. First, because the subconscious mind of man does not start existence from birth, and does not stop existing at death, it has a record of all events from antiquity. Second, in heaven time does not matter, since those existing there should be operating at speeds equal to or greater than c (the speed of light). Hence, since prophets are messengers from heaven, they operate at a different time to be able to relay the heavenly messages to those who live on earth.

When we ordinary mortals experience something, for prophets it has already passed in the spiritual realm. Likewise, anything that is in our future has already passed in heaven. That is why Jesus tells us that whatever we ask for from the Father, we should thank the Father as though we have already received it! The truth is that it was all done and finished in the spiritual world. You may ask, how is it that I don't have the things I want? The reason is simple: when one is not subconsciously in the right frame of mind, the tendency is to act contrary to the truths of the universe so that we may even drive away the things we need.

The laws of nature show that matter is neither created nor lost. This simply means that matter changes states. Since scientifically all matter is made up of atoms which in turn form complex molecules, living things are no exception. Therefore, it would mean that human beings do not start their existence at birth, but they have existed long before in another form as part of the universe. At death, people just change form. Their bodies are buried and will disintegrate into the component elements to join the various cycles of nature; while their spiritual part is untouchable and lives to perpetuity. If at creation God breathed His Spirit into humans to give them life, the Spirit of God that exists in them is invincible and therefore immune to death!

Sir Isaac Newton has formulated several laws of motion in physics. In one of these laws, speed is defined as distance covered in a certain amount of time. From this, it is evident that the fastest object would take the shortest period of time to cover a given distance under a defined set of conditions. If a certain distance is fixed between two (2) points A and B, anything that takes the shortest period or smallest time to cover this distance will be considered the fastest in a constant array of given conditions. This would mean that time taken to cover this defined distance shrinks as velocity increases. Hence, the time limit as things become faster between given distances is zero (0). Therefore, if something becomes so fast that it almost takes zero time to cover this distance, it would seem to be stationary at the finish point: even something that oscillates at speeds approaching, equal to or even greater than c (the speed of light), would seem stationary at the origin relative to the position of the observer. However, anything that is very slow to cover a given distance may seem to take forever to leave the starting point. Hence, the time limit as things become slower between given distances is infinity (∞). If the motion is circular, or the starting point is the finishing point, both the fastest and the slowest would seem to be stationary at the origin. The movement of something very slow is indiscernible, while the naked eye cannot detect the fastest of movements.

It is also important to realise that in life, time is a constant when referring to fixed scenarios. This simply means that the length of any minute will not be less or greater than sixty (60) seconds, and neither will a day be longer than twenty-four (24) hours. Hence, only the pace of events is the true variable. If a runner used to complete a mile in ten (10) minutes, but after some intensive training he runs the same distance in five (5) minutes, it means that his pace has increased so that he takes less time. However, this does not mean seconds have become any smaller; they are still the same. Hence time passes at a constant rate, but the pace of events changes in life. Two people may produce at a different magnitude in equal hours of work.

Life can only happen in the present. We are not able to live yesterday or tomorrow. We know what has happened in our past, we experience what is taking place in our present, but we do not know what will happen in our future. This is why it is very important for a person thriving in the present to do as much as possible by faith, hope, and love. Without this trio, nothing makes us hungry for the positive revelations brought by the future to our present. That is why many would make such claims as that we must live today as if it were our last day!

Let us imagine time as a conveyer belt whose breadth and length run to infinity. The future stretch of this belt is hidden from us. We can only see a small part of the belt as it passes through us in the present and quickly becomes the past as it deposits events into our present. Across and along the belt, all things that take place in life are randomly located at various intervals. The intervals can be interpreted in two dimensions (x and y). Anything that confronts us in life comes along this conveyer belt. For example, towards each person there may be good breaks, bad breaks, accidents, happiness, and even death. It may happen that an individual gets happiness after happiness or a bad break followed by a good one or mishap after mishap. There seem to be a lot of permutations. The only power controlling this conveyer belt and what it brings into our lives is the Creator of the universe working through our subconscious mind. The following diagram helps to demonstrate this contemplation.

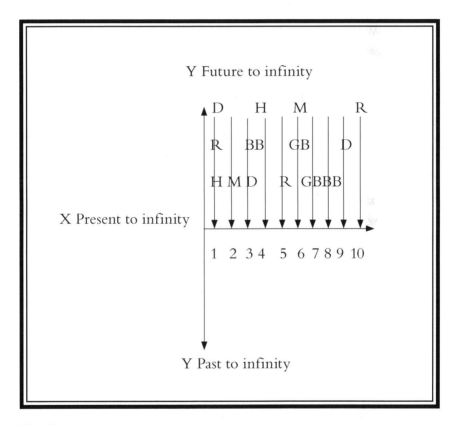

Fig. 2

In the diagram above, the conveyer belt of time runs from the future (*y* axis) and turns to the past at the present (*x* axis). Assume that all life happens along the *x* axis, since the area above the *x* axis represents the future, while that below depicts the past. The letter

D stands for death, H for happiness, M for marriage, R for riches, BB for bad break, and GB for good break. The downward arrows indicate the direction of each of the events as the time conveyer relays them towards different individuals 1, 2, 3, 4, 5, 6, 7, 8, 9, and 10 at the present. Note that person 1 may get happiness, riches, and death, while person 10 may get a bad break followed by riches. The intervals along the y axis indicate the length of time it may take for each of the events to come to an individual at the present. However, if the Creator were to shuffle the events, or the people were to change their positions along the x axis, the order of events happening in their lives would also change.

Ideally, every event that has gone through the present to the past is supposed to be deposited forever in the past. We are not supposed to relive the past, since it is gone and we cannot touch it. "But Paul (you ask), how come certain things which happened in the past are strongly influencing my life in the present?" Indeed, the past is the past! We only live with a record of the past events, and this arouses memories in us, bad or good, depending on the type and magnitude of each event.

The human mind arrests and stores events as they appear in the present. The longer the mind holds on to these events, the longer they become part of one's present and may even affect how one lives (some turn into habits). At times, other events may take place in our present and evoke memories and emotions of the past. The extent of these memories and what they do varies from one individual to another.

Also important is the magnitude of the impact of an event and how it is perceived by different individuals. For example, the world war and those who fought in the war are forever gone. Even if there are other world wars in the future, they will be different wars altogether. There may be similarities and resemblances, but these are different wars. However, as events take place that bear similarities with what confronted us in the past, memories are evoked that take us to the past. Many people always refer to "living in the past", which is impossible. The truth is that people arrest events which were supposed to have passed, but their brains refuse to let go and these events remain part of their present.

When a river flows downstream, it takes a whole lot of objects along. If one installed a filter of a certain pore size in the river, some objects would be retained by the filter, while others would pass and flow downstream. Note that unless the filter is removed, some things will always be trapped at the position of the filter in the river, and when the filter becomes overburdened, it will certainly rapture or burst.

Thus the river of time brings along many things in life. Some we arrest and keep as part of life in the present, while others we let go, to be deposited in the far past. However, the more we keep hurtful things and arrest them, we run the risk of our filters bursting. When this happens, some go into depression or other fatal states such as suicide or what some classify as irrational behaviour.

Through the years that I have studied natural science, I have only been able to appreciate the presence and greatness of God (Muslims may call Him Allah), the Creator of the universe. All discoveries by humans are brought about by time, which is controlled by our Father in heaven. This is clear from what Jesus says in the Scripture, that everyone should stay ready, for we do not know the time when the Son of Man will come. This day and hour is only known to the Father. It is also clear that not all is known to us, and some of our discoveries are bound to change the state of knowledge with time.

Although the Bible does not give an account of the stories of creation chronologically, that is merely because it is a document written and translated by people. Hence, like any written material, it will always contain human error. Neither does the Bible contain all the religious stories. This fact may simply be evident from the synoptic Gospels. The styles of the writers are different. The writings of Mathew, Mark, Luke, and John differ despite the similarity in their "overall" message. Hence, if we consider the overall message conveyed to us by the Bible, it is the number-one guidance tool in our lives. It inspires, it encourages, it comforts. It bears and relays the message of peace, good governance, but above all "hope, faith, and love." It is through positive interpretation and striving to practice this message that the world may become a better place to live in.

The Beginning

Chapter 1

The biblical story of creation in Genesis 1 tells us that when God first fashioned the universe, the earth did not have form and was uninhabited. There was complete darkness enveloping the powerful ocean that covered everything. The Spirit of God the Creator was moving over the water until He commanded that there be light—and light appeared through His word. In the beginning, the Word already existed; the Word was with God, and the Word was God (John 1: 1). The Word was the fountain of life, and this life brought light to humanity. Since then, the light has shown in the darkness and the latter has never been able to put it out (John 1: 5).

Before the birth of Christ our Lord, God sent His envoy—a man known as John the Baptist—to tell people about the light so that all could hear the message, believe, and prepare for the coming of the Messiah. John explained that he himself was not the light, but he bore the message about the light:

> This was the real light—the light that came into the world to shine on everyone. The Word that created everything was in the world in flesh form, and though God made everything through him, the world was blind and did not recognize him. (John 1: 9–10, TEV paraphrased)

This Scripture conveys a very important message: the Lord gives form to what is formless or without a definite shape. Before we took form in our mothers' wombs, we were amorphous until the Lord gradually gave us shape. Note that the Lord did not stop there; he even gives our lives shape and direction. Many of us look forward to establishing a good business, landing a good job, finding a good love relationship, or starting any project of our desire, but nothing seems to take shape. Why don't we call on the Creator of the universe? Remember, we have part of Him in us. If we remain connected with Him through our thoughts, we can command through His power vested in us, and things will be created in our lives as our subconscious becomes one and in harmony with Him.

There may be times when it seems that our lives are flooded by a raging ocean of anger, misfortune, and disappointment, but the Lord will give it meaning. Our circumstances may be engulfed in darkness, and we may not see any way out. However, we do not have to see but rather believe, since the Spirit of the Lord moves over the raging ocean of trouble in our lives and the law of life is the law of belief. We must live hopefully, faithfully, and righteously until the Lord commands, at the right time and place, for things to take form in our lives. "Let there be light" (Genesis 1: 3).

In John 8: 12 (NLT), the light that has come into the world speaks: "I am the light of the world. If you follow me, you won't have to walk in darkness, because you will have the light that leads to life." Also, in John 9: 39, Jesus said to a man who had just been healed from blindness, "I came to this world to judge so that the blind should see and those who see should become blind."

Remember, our eyes are able to see only if there is light. The majority of us think that because we hold certain educational qualifications, we see. However, we need the light that came from heaven into this world so we may truly see. In addition to our sensory eyes, we have other eyes—through our subconscious mind—that see beyond physical barriers. These eyes operate whether we are asleep or awake and are not confined by the limitations imposed by distance or time.

The beginning of true wisdom is the knowledge and respect for God. The Word of God is the source of life. It is through the Word that the universe was created and that all things are created in our lives. The Word brings light into our lives no matter how dark they may seem. Sometimes we go through such testing that some of us are overcome by the darkness, lose hope and faith in our Creator, and end up committing suicide.

We easily forget that He has created daylight to alternate with night. When it is night, we should learn to sleep and fill our subconscious minds with thoughts that will bring solutions. When things are dark, let us summon the One who brought light to humanity. This is the light that shines on everyone, drives away darkness, and brings hope in difficult times.

But we must be aware that our Father may not always answer prayer at our expected time. However, that does not mean He is not with us. We do not give our children whatever they ask for every time. We control what is good for them and may not give them what they are not yet ready for, lest they be harmed. We wait for the appropriate time. That is why David in Psalm 23: 4 asserted that even though he might walk through the valley of the shadow of death, he would not fear. Even when we go through the most testing times in life, we should choose faith over fear and trust in the Father, for He is with us and is greater than any challenge that may come our way. Let everyone choose faith in Him over fear.

The biggest challenge we have as humans is to recognize the Word and the Light and to believe that He who is in us is greater than our challenges. Throughout time, the Creator has sent His messengers to let us hear the Word and see the Light. But not all manage to do so. Some hear but do not understand, while others see but do not recognize. It is through earnest prayer and repentance from our sins that we may be granted true hearing and sight. On the other hand, even if we see and hear, we are not immune to spiritual testing. In the beginning, the Creator of the universe talked directly to humans and gave them clear instructions, so they had the choice to obey or disobey Him.

Adam and his wife, Eve, were put in the garden of Eden and instructed not to eat fruit from the tree of the knowledge of good and evil. Yet, they were tricked by the snake into breaking the Lord's instructions and ate the fruit. It is worth noting that God had told Adam and Eve that they would die on the same day if they ate the fruit, but the snake told them that God did not want them to be like Him by having knowledge of what is good and bad. It is amazing to see how the human heart always desires to reach the greatest possible status. Everybody wants to be somebody.

This desire creates fights in workplaces where subordinates long to occupy the posts of their bosses. This same desire causes much confusion in churches and other organizations and even leads to the splitting of institutions. If we are not satisfied by what the Lord has given us, praying for guidance towards our God-created purpose, we keep fighting to be like others. Desiring to be great is good, but the path we take to greatness is what matters. If we choose the wrong path, we may end up losing what our Master has planned for our future.

In Matthew 25: 14–30, Jesus teaches about talents. It is not true that the third man who supposedly buried his talent did nothing. The truth is that he worked contrary to his God-given purpose by wanting to be like someone else. In my study of reproduction biology, I learned that in the process of meiosis, chromosomal material is shuffled during differentiation so that no individual may be a true copy of another. The reality is that the snake was jealous of the love God had for His people, Adam and his wife. So the serpent used the desires of their hearts to make them sin against the Lord.

The Bible says that, after talking to the snake, Eve noticed how beautiful the fruit was. Her desire was heightened, and she felt more and more like eating the fruit until she was overcome with desire and finally ate it. She then gave some to her husband. Most times when we are about to do what we are not supposed to, we have a myriad of thoughts trying to convince us why it would be good to do it as well as reasons not to do it. The only way to overcome this conflict is through prayer and giving the Lord space to make the decision on our behalf. This we may achieve by not concentrating on the wrong thoughts, thereby strongly forming an inward impression that they should come to pass. Our Father loves us and will not lead us the wrong way. His plans are not our plans, and we have to trust that He plans righteously, for He unconditionally loves us. In team building, people are taught to trust one another with their lives. So why can't people trust their Creator with their lives? Is easier to trust men than God with our lives?

Immediately after eating the fruit, Adam and Eve realized that they were naked. How many of us do things we are not supposed to do and instantly feel remorse after we have done them? We feel sorry after we have engaged in fighting, after we have fallen to adulterous deeds, after we have stolen from someone, or after we have killed someone. After the deed is done, we discover our nakedness. But instead of repenting, we start building our defence and trying to cover up our disobedience so that we will not be discovered or seen. The truth is that we cannot hide ourselves from the only supernatural force that controls everything.

The Lord asked Adam, "Where are you, my beloved creation?" Adam explained that he heard the Lord walking in the garden, he was afraid, and he hid because he was naked. Then the Lord continued to ask Adam, "Who told you that you are naked?" It is common for us as people to hide when we feel that we have done something bad and to want to be seen when we feel that we have done something that we feel is praiseworthy and may somehow add to our glory. Today where are most of us spiritually? Are we hiding among the trees, for we have disobeyed the Lord? Have we impregnated some girl, stolen from someone, or done anything that we ought not to have done, and are we blaming others for it? Adam blamed the woman, and the woman blamed the snake! No one wanted to take responsibility. Let us repent and ask for forgiveness. Then the Lord pronounced His judgement: Adam and his wife forfeited the garden of Eden as part of their punishment. They had to move out of their blessing place.

Today many of us cry out that we are not blessed. Let us look into what we have done to forfeit the Lord's glory and blessings. Are we spiritually where He needs us? Have we genuinely repented and truly asked for His forgiveness? He is the Lord; His love is eternal, and it endures forever; He is the Creator of the universe, and all things are known to him. He wants us to humble ourselves before Him and acknowledge that without Him we are nothing and that there is nothing we can do by our might. If we pray: "Lord, You know the desires of my heart, good and bad. Please guide me along the right trail, as I know You will always make superior choices for me."

As leaders and rulers of this world we sometimes sin against the Father through committing undesirable deeds to humankind. Then, instead of openly apologizing and asking for forgiveness, we want to cling onto our positions and consider apologizing to be a weakness. Then we start passing thorny laws. The truth is that the more we try and cover ourselves up in lies and defence, the more exposed we become as our integrity fades. Children often put their hands on their faces and think that they are hiding.

The Bible says that Abel was a shepherd, while Cain became a farmer. These two were sons of Adam and Eve, and they followed different career paths. They also differed in how they presented their offerings to the Lord. While Abel offered the best parts of one of his lambs to the Lord, and this was accepted, Cain's harvest was not acceptable. It is not that the Lord did not like Cain, but He resented how he presented his gift. Perhaps Cain's heart was not fully committed to the offering, or he might have offered without respect, as if the Lord were his companion. Cain's nature is revealed from the way he later answered the Lord when he was asked about where his brother was. Cain answered that he was not supposed to take care of his brother.

The answer is that we do have to take care of our brothers and sisters all the time. We came into this world with the purpose of serving others. Our brothers and sisters are not only those with whom we share the same parents, but all humankind. If we become offended through jealousy by what our brothers do, let us not kill them but support and even learn from them how it is done. Their success becomes ours as long as we keep a positive attitude and understand that we are Jehovah's team.

This team is called the believers, and it is constantly playing against Satan's team (e.g., the pagans or the godless). Note that the game strategy for believers is prayer, love, truth, trustworthiness, wisdom, peace, hope, faith, repentance, humility, mercy, forgiveness, … and persistence in their purest form. However, the pagans' strategy and goal is to turn these qualities around and let them fade to nothingness.

It is worth noting that after a punishment was put on Cain, he complained that it was too hard to endure. He certainly did not think that what he had done to his brother was painful to bear! His brother begged him to stop, but he could not. The killers, hijackers, and rapists of our day ignore their victims' pleas for them to stop. However, when courts of law announce heavy judgements on them, they think it is unjust. Is this really how selfish we sometimes become?

Although Cain had been punished, whoever was to lay a hand on him would be punished seven times more. This is why it becomes important that we should not take revenge on those who have wronged us, since in doing so we seven times burden ourselves with their sin through the scientific laws through which our minds operate. How many acts of revenge have we committed, blowing our chances for a fulfilled life? The moment we think on revenge, we begin a process of impressing our brains with evil thoughts, and soon we are no different from the criminals who hurt us.

In the beginning, when human wickedness had spread over the world, the Lord became sorry that he ever created people. However, the Lord was pleased with Noah. Noah was instructed to build a boat so that he and all that was in the boat would be safe during the flood. Today we may be facing different floods such as joblessness, abuse, starvation and poverty, inability to have children, drug abuse, wars, and many other troubles that threaten our lives. Like Noah, we can float during these difficult times if we use prayer as our boat. A boat is not built overnight or in times of danger when situations threaten to take our lives. It should be something we always have ready. We do not buy a first-aid kid or start frantically running around looking for one when in trouble; instead, we keep one ready for times of emergency. We must not cease to pray even when the flood is over. Praying constantly makes us stronger, and we float easily whenever confronted with uneasy situations.

After the flood, Noah offered a sacrifice to the Lord. This could have been a way of saying, "Thank You, Lord, for sparing our lives and sustaining us through the dreadful times of the flood." How many of us do realize the importance of giving thanks to the Lord? After conquering difficult times and coming into happiness, do we realize it was not by our wisdom and power, but by the grace of the Father? I know that some of us have prayed hard during difficult times and even hung on every sermon in our church, but as soon as our lives turn around positively, we must remember not to wander from the Lord. Following the sacrifice, the Lord promised that He would never again destroy all living beings by flood and that there would be time for planting and time for harvest, there would be cold and hot times, summer and winter, and there would be day and night (Genesis 8: 22).

When many of us go through hard times, we tend to forget that there is time for planting and time for harvest. The seeds do not germinate on the same day they are planted and start bearing fruit. It takes time for a seed to germinate as a shoot, grow, mature, and bear fruit. From germination to bearing fruit, there is a certain progression that is required. In life, before realizing the Lord's blessings, we need to mature spiritually and develop enough strength to sustain the result of our blessing. If the fruits are heavy and the stem is weak, then the stem will break even before the fruit is ripe. By the time any plant starts bearing fruit, the roots have also acquired necessary depth and strength. If the root system is weak, the plant becomes top-heavy and falls over. The situation is even worse in windy conditions.

Those who are quickly blessed, before they have an in-depth understanding about the Lord and His ways, always run the risk of forgetting and turning away from Him. Some may even become arrogant and grow into a great nuisance to society. When the winds of change blow and storms of life charge, without deep-rooted faith, some are bound to falter and collapse under the burdens that the world lays on them.

In botany I learned about *viviparity* in salty marshland ecosystems. Here germination takes place before seeds are dispersed. For example, in many mangroves the seedling germinates and grows under its own energy while still attached to its parent. This is important, because if the seeds are dispersed before they develop into seedlings with roots, they may not be able to germinate and survive in the salty soils.

When it is cold and dark, there is not much activity. In winter, plants are dormant, and they will come to life in spring, while some animals hibernate until summer sets in. At night humans are supposed to sleep because it is dark and they cannot see what they are doing. There are times in our lives when it is cold and we are struggling; other times it is warm and a lot seems to be going according to plan. At night it is dark and we may not seem to find our way. However, we are sustained by the fact that we know the rays of the sun will cut off the blanket of darkness at dawn and warm us with hope.

It may be dark in your life today, but remember, the Lord promised that night will alternate with day. In your family it may be cold and dry now, but summer will soon set in with hissing rains, and the warmth, humidity, and dampness will commend themselves to your senses. You will soon shake off the blanket of hibernation and move freely! Remember, when insects undergo metamorphosis, all the stages are necessary, and they cannot skip any of them to complete their life cycle. Noah and his sons were given a new beginning and a new hope of having many children by multiplying and spreading all over the world. To you, my brother and sister, a new hope of prosperity and abundant wealth is still not ruled out.

Later the descendants of Noah wanted to work against the Lord's will of multiplying and spreading all over the world. They started building a city with a tower that would reach the sky. They wanted to make a name for themselves. There is nothing wrong with building structures as long as they are in favour of the Lord and they are meant for His glory. Hence, if we do things for our own glory and we boast and become arrogant, our Father in heaven becomes displeased.

See also Isaiah 14: 12–15 (TEV):

> King of Babylonia, bright morning star, you have
> fallen from heaven! In the past you conquered nations,
> but now you have been thrown to the ground. You
> were determined to climb up to heaven and to place
> your throne above the highest stars. You thought you
> would sit like a king on that mountain in the north
> where the gods assemble. You said you would climb
> to the tops of the clouds and be like the Almighty. But
> instead, you have been brought down to the deepest
> part of the world of the dead.

The king of Babylon exalted and glorified himself but then was made lowly. Similarly, Satan (Lucifer) exalted and glorified himself, wanted to lead the assembly and preside over the heavenly beings, but was cast out of heaven.

Those who built the city and tower of Babylon were made to speak in different languages and they were confused and scattered all over the world. Our lives may be disgruntled and our goals distorted as long as they are not in line with the will of the Father—although sometimes through the hardships the Lord may be developing certain qualities in us that are important for our future. It is for those who seek not their own glory but that of the Father that it is written, great rewards await them in heaven. "A person who speaks on his own authority is trying to gain glory for himself. But he who wants glory for the one who sent him is honest, and there is nothing false in him" (John 7:18 TEV)."

In the earlier discussion about time, we saw that only the Creator in heaven can change the location of a person in life, and we saw how important this change may be in determining what the future brings to individuals. Because the Father knows what the future will bring to the present, He commanded His servant Abram in Genesis 12 to leave his country and relatives and his father's household to journey to a foreign land. It was in this foreign land where Abram would receive blessings meant for him. In the foreign land of Canaan, Abram travelled until he came to the sacred tree of Moreh, the holy place at Shechem.

The movement or position shift we take in life need not only be physical. We may need to make a spiritual move to change our wicked ways. Those who abuse drugs need to leave their drug-abusing friends and drug lots. Those who are committed to other people's families through adulterous ways, lust, and fornication should move to their own families and rekindle the fires of love and peace. Those who occupy undeserved positions should move to where they should be. It is time for those who steal to abandon the act and return what they have unlawfully taken and for those who hold grudges to forgive and let go.

The Lord is commanding us today to move to the land of Canaan, to the holy place at Shechem where we can worship and build Him an altar. Our blessings are awaiting us in the land designated by the Lord. Hence, let us move to a spiritually correct frame of mind. Some may say that they have done all things necessary, but their troubles have not left them. Note the specificity of the location. First you have to reach Canaan; in Canaan go to Shechem; and in Shechem find the holy place at Moreh! We must acknowledge the presence of our Father in heaven, love Him genuinely, turn away from our sins, and serve Him through our service to humankind. Once we have obeyed the Lord and we are where He wants us, He will hold back none of our deserved blessings.

In Genesis 15:1, the Lord promised to shield Abram and to give him a great reward. However, Abram did not see how this would come to pass. Abram looked at his present status then and thought that it would not change. He judged the situation by human scales. He and Sarai did not have children, and he did not think they ever would. He predicted his future based on his current situation and what he had learned from the past. He forgot that the times and the occasions are under the Lord's command. The Lord took him outside and made him try to "number" (name) the stars. After being taken out, Abram agreed with the Lord, who was pleased with Abram's trust. Sometimes we need to be taken outside the scope of our minds, outside our current thinking and location, outside what we have learned from the professors of the world, outside what the statistics predict, so that we may see new visions of the Lord and what He is capable of doing for us.

I grew up in the most rural part of Lesotho in Southern Africa. My family lived in abject poverty. Most of my brothers and sisters could not go beyond their high school education. My future also looked bleak. I never thought I would have a university degree; the very idea was far-fetched. However, I had to leave the land of my birth, my friends, my relatives, and my neighbours in order to get my education. Later my whole family had to move to an urban area where it would be easy to look after them now that all their children had moved. The reality is that our Father in heaven had a plan for us to move to this new location in order for our lives to change.

New locations bring new thinking and approaches to life. Sometimes we feel so trapped where we are that we do not see how any positive change may come. We are so used to our locations that they impose a ceiling to what we may and may not do. We do not have to see it through the eyes of our senses; the Lord sees it, and we have to join Him through spiritual eyes. There is no limit to His possibilities!

As long as we stay in faith and live by faith, there is nothing that Jehovah may not change for us, but we have to obey Him and always act according to His plan. This is the basis on which the Lord made a covenant with Abram and changed his name to Abraham. The Lord promised to give Abraham and his descendants the land of Canaan forever on the condition that they would keep the agreement. Hence, the blessings that we receive from the Father in heaven will keep flowing as long as we stay faithful and truthful to Him. The covenant between Abraham and the Lord was sealed by circumcision.

Sarai's name was also changed to Sarah, since she would be a mother to nations, and there would be kings among her descendants. Please note that to Abraham and his wife it seemed impossible that they would have a child at their age. In our lives today many prospects seem unlikely or even impossible according to our judgement. Let us dare to dream big, for nothing is too big for the Creator of the universe to do. He created the flesh of Abraham and his wife, and therefore He knew when that flesh would be fertile and when it would not. He knows the material of which He made the flesh, He set its time limit, and He knows when it will wear out. He derived the set constants and variables of the model that governs fertility; hence He can re-alter constraints on that same model however He wishes.

Today we largely rely on scientific predictions based on limited models derived by our inferior minds before we act on ideas that seem risky. We forget that the predictions have to do with the universe created by the Lord, who holds and drives the one true universal model that can predict accurately. Moreover, He can and may change any variable or constant to influence outcomes of universal events, whether existent or non-existent, at any given point in space and time, either in this life or the next. It is good to plan and use technology to make our predictions, but we must not forget that the Lord is the realtor.

There are times when farmers stop planting because it has been predicted that there would be no rain. However, if they would plough their fields and ask the Father for rain, there would be rain! Abraham and his wife looked at their age as an indication that they would not have a child; even when the Lord promised them a child, they laughed in disapproval. Human nature is such that we believe and base our lives and predictions mostly on what time has brought into our present. We rely too much on human knowledge and mortal professors. Let us not forget the immortal and eternal Professor who accurately sees into and knows what the future brings our way. Let us also not forget that after He fashioned our flesh, He gave us His Spirit. Therefore through His Spirit we have Him in us. If we embark on the process to discover the powers we have through the One who resides in us, there is no limit to what we can do.

In Genesis 18 Abraham invites, welcomes, and prepares a meal for three strangers. He goes through a great deal of trouble to make them feel at home. After the men have eaten the food he has served, one of them says that he will come back nine months later, as Sarah will have a son. What is intriguing is the fact that one of the three men was the Lord. He had brought Abraham and Sarah a child that very same day, but they did not realize it.

Sometimes the Lord brings what we want right before our eyes but if not guided by the Holy Spirit, we may not be able to see it. The seed planted in Sarah's womb was certainly not wholly of this world. She would give birth to one of the heavenly creatures implanted by the Lord Himself.

We also learn the importance of being good to everyone regardless of their status. Abraham and Lot treated strangers with love and respect and took good care of them. Their good hearts could not go unrewarded. Abraham received a son, and Lot was saved from death during the destruction of Sodom. Abraham's son was born when the Lord said he would be, and he was named Isaac. This baby boy brought great joy to Abraham's family. It is a great promise that those who stay faithful, no matter how old they are and how dark situations may be, will always receive His blessings. Today others may be lying in bed sick, with their medical reports looking depressing, but the Lord will pull them out as long as they believe and maintain good faith. It may look like there is no money to send our children to school, but they will attend school at the time the Lord promised they will.

If we refer to diagram 2, we may say Lot was shifted along the line in his present to be saved from death that was coming his way. The two strangers he welcomed into his house (the angels) told him to take everything that belonged to him and leave Sodom. However, to Abraham and Sarah the conveyer belt of time brought joy through the birth of Isaac, while at the same time the birth of this boy brought a difficult time for Hagar and her son, Ishmael, who had to leave the comfort of Abraham's home. As the unknown future unfolds, it presents us with different actions of varying impact and duration. How we respond to these circumstances under the Lord's guidance is crucial in determining what becomes of us.

What has time brought you, and how are you responding? Remember, the darkest night of all is perceived to be the day when one faces death. I like the words of Marley in the book *Old Marley and the Boy* that I once read while I was in secondary school. Marley tells the boy that a man can only cry when he feels that his heart is going to break. The reality is that there are times when the future unfolds to bombard us with events that make us collapse. These are occasions and moments when the hand of the Lord can work miracles.

In our daily language we often say that we should let the past be the past. The truth is that, although time has passed, events of differing magnitude have been deposited into our brains, where they will stay with us until the brain dies. The emotions roused by these events depend on how serious an individual brain assesses them to be.

Hence, certain events are easily forgettable for some while not for others. Some events are recorded as indelible scars on certain human brains, while others are like mere faded pencil lines.

In the desert on the way to Shur, the angel of the Lord met Hagar and asked her where she came from and where she was going. Hagar answered that she was running away from her master, but the angel commanded her to go back and be a slave. We may not avoid events that the Lord has planned to take effect in our lives by running away. Are you running away from your troubles today? Have they treated you unfairly at work and you have decided to quit? Are you willing to go back to these unfair conditions for the sake of the Lord? At times we have to trust Him enough to be prepared to be fools and even die for our faith. As the apostle Paul writes in his first letter to the Corinthians, the foolishness of the Lord is wiser than human wisdom. Hence, if time brings an event to our present that is meant to shape us for our unknown future, it is a mistake to avoid it, lest we not be completely shaped for our intended destiny.

It is at this time—when everything possible to our minds has faded away—that the Master steps in. In the wilderness of Beersheba, when all her hope was gone and there was no water, Hagar left the child, sat about a hundred metres away, and began to cry. She could not see herself surviving the conditions. What is happening in your life today? Have the odds turned so that you are wandering alone in the wilderness of Beersheba? Is all the water gone—you have no food and clothes in the house, no money to send children to school, perhaps even no house to live in, and all those you trusted have turned against you? Do your earthly masters no longer find a need to keep you around?

Perhaps you cannot bear to see your child die. The child may represent your various dreams in life, but the most important child you must be on guard not to lose is your faith and hope. Have you lost your faith and hope and left them under some tree a hundred metres away? It is time to turn to the Lord. The Lord knows you and your challenges. He knows what each and every one of us is called for. None of us has become part of the universe by mistake. He guards us around the clock throughout our lifetime, and He never goes to sleep! His love for every individual is never a function of how we think of each other.

The angel of the Lord told Hagar not to be afraid, for the Lord had heard the boy Ishmael crying from under the tree. It is at this time that I remember the biblical saying that our hairs are counted and that people should not worry about who will provide for them. The birds of heaven do not sow or reap but are always provided for. Indeed, we are much more worth than the various components of biodiversity.

The angel commanded Hagar to get up, pick up her child, and comfort him. I invite you to pick up your dreams and work on them, for our Father will open your eyes to see the well. Indeed, rekindle your faith and hope. There is a well of life next to you, but you may not see it because the Lord has not opened your eyes. Remember, in the beginning there was light, and the light was God. It is only through the light that we may see. Even though you may live in the wilderness of Paran, the Lord will make you grow up spiritually into a skilful hunter in your dreams of life.

The Lord has heard you crying, and he will come through for you! He will pick you up and comfort you! He has the water of life! Not even the smallest of birds may abandon its chicks when they cry for help. So how much more is our Father in heaven willing to do for us?

In the news these days on television, in newspapers, and over the radio, there are stories of women and girls who throw away their children and men who are on a rape spree. Some are mothers under stress who do not see how they will provide for their babies. Others do it for selfish purposes.

I would like to reach out to you today. Those children have not been born by mistake! The Lord has a plan for them; otherwise He would have not allowed them to come. Pray that He opens your eyes to see. He has heard and He continues to hear the cries of those babies from rubbish pits, toilets, and other unworthy locations where they have been dumped. He continues to hear the cries of those who are raped and killed.

Let us pray that He gives us strength through hard times and that He gives us faith, hope, and love. We should learn to live in unconditional love for the Lord and for one another. The hard times we go through are just a test, and they are meant to promote us. Really, it is the hardships that turn the screws in our lives and mould us into better beings.

The Lord commanded Abraham to go to Moriah to offer his only beloved son as a sacrifice to Him. Abraham did not even ask a question but acted on blind faith. He went on to prepare for the sacrifice. His son was asking him questions about the lamb for the offering. Abraham's heart must have sunk, and his spirit must have been vexed, but his faith, love, and obedience for the Lord kept him going. He made the boy Isaac to carry the wood. When Isaac asked about an animal for the offering, Abraham's answer was that the Lord would provide the lamb. When they arrived at the location for the sacrifice, Abraham tied up his son and placed him on the wood which was upon the altar he had built. When Abraham was about to lay a hand on his son, the Lord stopped him and showed him a ram.

This was a very tough test, but it is interesting to see that Abraham named that place "The Lord Provides." Indeed the Lord provides in times of hardship! At such a time many of us would have become disillusioned with our faith and lost hope, but for every moment, every second, Abraham remained steadfast and kept his faith with obedience. Then the Lord made a vow to bless Abraham after he had passed this toughest of tests.

I cannot help wondering what would have happened if Abraham had offered his son. Remember the Lord had promised Abraham would be a father of nations, but we also know that all nations are children of the Lord. In the New Testament, we see the Lord offering His only beloved son to set nations free from sin. Then it becomes clear that this type of sacrifice could only be offered by the Lord and that it had been pre-planned in heaven. If Abraham had gone through with it, he would have assumed the position of the heavenly Father. Then, in later years, the children of Israel would argue and exalt their father Abraham to the position of the Lord, for he too would have sacrificed his only son Isaac.

This sacrifice was also a prophecy showing what the Lord would do through His Son for the liberation of sinful humanity. That He would be made to carry a wooden cross to Golgotha where he would be sacrificed for the freedom of us all! When Abraham answered that the Lord would provide a lamb for the sacrifice, he did not realize that he was prophesying that in the future the Lord would provide His Lamb to be sacrificed on the cross (altar) at Calvary! Indeed it was during this time that Abraham witnessed what would happen to the Son of Man—for in John 8: 56 Jesus confirms to the Jews that their father Abraham wanted to see His day, indeed saw it, and was glad. They were baffled at how He could know of Abraham when He was not even fifty years of age. How much do we love Him? How much do we obey Him? Do we hold back our faith and hope in Him? The reality is that He loves us more than we love ourselves! That is why He kept his promise to His servant Abraham and gave to him two nations at the same time through Isaac and Rebecca, in their sons, Esau and Jacob.

Sometimes the Lord tests us so intensely that if we are not well-rooted in faith, we end up making serious mistakes and taking wrong decisions. Esau grew up to become a skilful hunter while Jacob became a farmer. One day when Esau came from hunting, he was extremely hungry and asked Jacob for a meal. Jacob explained that he could only trade off his meal for Esau's rights as the firstborn son (Gen. 25:27–34). Since Esau could not endure the pangs of hunger, he sold his rights for food. This reminds me of our youth who often lose their integrity for a ride in a fabulous car, an outing, or a meal in some restaurant or hotel. Please, let us not be naïve. The Lord has already supplied these things in our lives at the right time. We are capable of obtaining these things from our Father. Each and every one of us is a complete, dignified human with a clear mandate from Him.

I know many people who think that they are desperate, and they are in a tight corner where they cannot escape. Hence, they think that they are compelled into making a bad choice. Will your partner or friend leave you if you do not do something risky or unintelligent for them? Do you feel compelled to get into drugs because your friends think it is cool? Are you in a position to lose your job because your bosses want you to be involved in illegal actions? Are you going to do something stupid because your family will go without food or even leave your husband for men who have money? Are you out in the streets selling your body in order to make a living? Do those politicians want to use you to do their dirty work, and are you going to do it for money? Remember that the Lord created you in His image! You are far more important to Him than food and money.

In Matthew 6: 25 Jesus tells us not to be worried about the food and drink we need in order to survive or about the clothes we need to cover and make our bodies presentable. He is highlighting that life is more precious than food, and He goes on to say that the body is worth more than clothes. Indeed none of us can extend our life by brooding over our troubles. The Lord wants us to keep our integrity and live in discipline and self-respect.

When the tests we come through are over, we will get our marks and be promoted, depending on how well we have done. For those who are familiar with the education system, they know that the tests given at primary school are not the same as those in high school, and neither are those in high schools the same as those at colleges or universities. Which test are you taking today? Are you willing to write it and pass? Then do not give in easily. Your teacher is right beside you, if you calm down and pray you will remember what He has taught you, and he will shine the light that will make you see everything vividly.

Throughout my years at school, students dropped out at different levels. Some became dropouts from primary school, others from high school, and others from college. However, there are people who have made it to the final level of their education path—although education never stops as long as we live. It was also evident that the tests and examinations were given at particular times during the academic calendar. The whole year was never a test or exam period. Hence, the tests and exams were temporary in nature. Within the three or so hours that students were given to write their exams, they had to endure and display their moral fibre and stamina. Then the whole superficial trauma would be over. It is amazing how soon some of us give up when confronted with challenges in life. Note that as there are different subjects at school for which an exam is given, there are many challenges to go through in life for which a test or exam is taken in the spiritual realm.

Let us not give in to bad desires and take routes that lead to disastrous lives. Not only had Esau given away the birthright that the Lord had bestowed on him; he also forfeited his father Isaac's final blessing. If we do not truly repent, the choices we make today may affect our lives in the future, for if our actions disappoint the Lord, we force Him to shuffle things in our future so that we don't get His favour. Esau only realized his mistakes too late, and instead of asking for redemption, he was filled with rage towards his brother. The habit of looking for quick-fix measures and get-rich-quick schemes are like moths eating through the fibre of our society today.

Through life, I have learned that sometimes the difference between winners and failures in life depends on how we spend our present time and on what we constantly think. One day I met a young man who was saying that he drinks beer to get rid of boredom and pass the time. Then I told him that time has no beginning or end. If he was doing unworthy things trying to make time pass, he was only wasting effort.

At first the young man looked amazed and short of words. Then he glowed with happiness and began to see the importance and power of making correct choices as it dawned on him that the present is an infinitesimally small amount of time where the future is suddenly becoming the past. I hope the Lord today helps you into making the right options. All things are possible in Him, for He created everything, He gave us life, and that life has purpose. Otherwise you could not be alive. I invite you to fully live your life for Him and find your new purpose in Him.

When Jacob was sent off to sojourn with his uncle Laban in Mesopotamia, on his journey he came to a holy place and camped, laying his head on a stone. During this time he was troubled as he was running away from his brother Esau who wanted to kill him. Sleeping with one's head laid on a stone is not at all comfortable. There are many occasions in our lives where life deals us a bad hand, and we feel as if we are laying our heads on stone. Some are in abusive relationships; others are accused of crimes they did not commit, while others do not have bread on their tables. Some at this moment are dealing with a loss of their loved ones, while others have been dumped and they feel rejected. Do not think it's acceptable to attempt to kill yourself. Rather, it is very important to see that in this uncomfortable position was where Jacob communicated with the Lord for the first time. In this testing position for sleep, he had a divine dream, and this is where he discovered that through him nations would be blessed.

When we go through difficult times and it feels as if we have stones for pillows, very often we doubt the existence of the Lord and we think that He has forsaken us, and some of us end up embarking on paths that lead to wrong journeys. Please note what Jacob said after he had had a mysterious dream, "The Lord is here! He is in this place, and I didn't know it! ... What a terrifying place this is! It must be the house of God; it must be the gate that opens into heaven" (Gen. 28: 16–17, TEV). Your miserable place and position today may be an important chance for you to meet with the Lord; it may be the gate that opens into your blessing, your future, and your spiritual life. If Jacob hadn't left his home, although it was a painful flight, he might not have come to the holy place at Bethel. Let us make a vow with the Lord, that if He protects us through these difficult times we are going through in the journey of life, if He gives us food and clothing, then He is our Father and Lord, and we will serve Him. Let us set up a spiritual ensign as Jacob erected a memorial stone.

Jacob's struggle did not end at Bethel. During the twenty years he stayed at Laban's he encountered tempering challenges. He toiled seven years to get his uncle's daughter Rebecca for a wife, but he was cheated into marrying her elder sister Leah. However, because he worked towards a pleasing target, the additional seven years he had to work were like a short time to him. He spent the last six years working to earn his wealth. In the end he fled from his uncle, for there was no longer harmony between them. The Lord commanded Jacob to go back to the land of his fathers. The Lord was working on Jacob's behalf, for He had seen the injustices done to him by his uncle.

As long as we stay faithful to Him, our Father in heaven knows exactly when it is payback time. You might have worked very hard and faithfully in the past without being appreciated; instead, you ended up losing your job. Some have even been rewarded with insults. There will be payback time. The Lord will not let people wrong you and get away with it. This does not mean that we must wish doom on those who do us wrong. I know a number of people who were laid off from their work because they were faithful. Some have simply been gotten rid of because they are not affiliates to certain political parties.

Jacob had crossed the Jordan with nothing but a walking stick as he plainly says in Genesis 32: 10. By the time he fled from Laban he was a rich man with herds, wives, and children. On his way back, after sending all that he owned across the River Jabbok, Jacob remained behind. At that same night a man came and wrestled with him. When the man saw that he was not winning the battle, he struck Jacob on the hip and asked Jacob to let him go. Even with a limping hip, Jacob refused to let go unless he was blessed. The man blessed Jacob and told him he would be named Israel, for he had struggled with the Lord and with men and won (Gen. 32: 22–32)!

Sometimes we give up too soon. If Jacob had let go and cried that his hip was hurting, he wouldn't have got the blessing. He was tested hard before the blessing was given. A man who was to become father to the Lord's people needed to be a tough and enduring one, not frail and fragile. Most people like huge responsibilities, but they don't want to be tried and tested. Indeed, nothing but discipline and endurance kept Jacob going on. Many would have given up, complaining about how the ache in their hip was, but he endured until the blessing came forth.

During my years at school I learned about properties of metals. Tenacity is one of the most important qualities depending on where a metal is going to be used. Other metals are to be used in extremely hot and cold conditions, and they need to behave well under these stressing conditions. If these metals are not prepared as required, their lack of proper strength may lead to disasters. Likewise, huge responsibilities in our lives come with huge testing to prepare us for future victories. Foundations prepared for skyscrapers differ significantly from those prepared for single-roomed flat structures.

When Jacob met his brother, Esau, he demonstrated spiritual maturity. He bowed down to his brother, humbled himself, and said that he was nothing but a servant to his brother; as a result, they were reconciled. He had come through trouble and he was seasoned. He was ready for that part of his life. Sometimes our pride destroys our chance to lead peaceful lives. Jacob knew that if he humbled himself in front of a character like Esau and gave him seniority as his brother's heart desired, he would win his favour, which was the victory that mattered.

Jacob was instructed to go and live at Bethel in Canaan. He was named Israel and told that nations would descend from him and that he would be an ancestor to kings. Bethel seems to be a place where the Lord had chosen to bless Jacob. As long as Jacob would remain in agreement with Him, all his blessings would come through there.

Sometimes we hold on to wrong places and miss the Lord and His blessings, for He has not prepared to bless us there. We refuse to move, but we have seen in diagram 2 how important it is to be moved by the Lord. Sometimes the wrong places we occupy are not merely physical but spiritual as well. If we stay in the wrong frame of mind, if we do not abandon our jealousy, anger, hatred, immorality, theft, laziness, and drugs, then we have not come to our Bethel where the Lord wants us to be in order to enjoy His blessings.

Imagine if someone who is always helplessly drunk would be allowed to drive a beautiful car worth millions. Surely no one would allow that to happen. The Lord knows exactly when we are ready to be given responsibilities and when to bless us. If we are spiritually drunk, He may not entrust huge responsibilities to us, lest we cause unnecessary catastrophes.

As Jacob continued to live in Canaan with his family, he had his sons looking after his herds. Sometimes they behaved irresponsibly. Joseph, their younger brother, disliked their bad behaviour and brought bad reports to his father about them. His father favoured him and made a long robe for him. Joseph's brothers hated him for their father's prominent love on him and for his mysterious dreams. One day Jacob send Joseph to Shechem where his brothers were taking care of the flock to see if all was okay. As Joseph went after his brothers to Dothan, they saw him from a distance and plotted to kill him. As he came up to his brothers, they ripped off his robe and threw him into a dry well. However, through Judah's advice they ended up selling him to an Ishmaelite caravan, which took him to Egypt. The brothers killed a goat and soaked Joseph's robe in it to convince their father that a wild animal had killed him (Gen. 37).

Joseph's brothers hated him because he was the chosen one. Throughout the process of ripping off his robe and selling him, Joseph was quiet like a lamb. The Bible does not tell us of him saying any word or fighting back. His brothers were jealous of his divine gift from the Lord. They did not realize that he would save the tribes of Israel from famine in the future. The story of Joseph is a prophecy showing what would happen in Israel in the future. What happened to Joseph demonstrated how the Messiah would be rejected by His own people for not approving of their behaviour and telling them the truth about the Father. The Messiah would be rejected by His own people. They would tear his robe to pieces, and it would be soaked in His blood. He would be sold for pieces of silver, and yet He would have come to save these people. He would be bringing them the real bread from heaven. However, during all His torment, He would be silent before His torturers.

When Joseph arrived at Shechem, he could not find his brothers because they had moved to Dothan. Jacob had sent Joseph to take food to his brothers, and he expected to find them at Shechem. In life we shift our location sometimes to miss the Lord's plan and His blessings. Joseph's brothers were lucky enough to find someone like him, who went after them even though they had moved to Dothan.

In Joseph we find the qualities of the Lord's messenger. He is persistent, enduring, and loving. He follows through to see that his father's errand is fulfilled. Likewise the Messiah followed through with His Father's mission although it was difficult. He went after the lost sheep of Israel to bring them to the Father.

Are you facing difficulties today? Are you still at Shechem where the messenger of the Lord should find you? Are you staying in faith, hope, and the love of the Lord? Have you not spiritually moved to Dothan? Perhaps you have given up, moved to drugs, moved to abusive ways, given up on praying, moved to all kinds of wickedness, and have committed adultery.

In our lives the Lord talks to us through His messengers whom we often reject and call names. Joseph was called a dreamer and accused of wanting to rule over his brothers. In this, there is also an analogy with the story and life of the Messiah, and the saying that "the stone rejected by builders has become the most important of all" is starting with Joseph. Although he was thrown away, sold to Egypt, he would be important in times of famine, and his ideas would save the people. At work, in your family, or in your organisation, you might be rejected for your dreams and ideas; you might be the most disliked. Look deep into yourself; what are the signs? Pray that the

Lord will give you an answer. Maybe you will lead your people through difficult times.

In Egypt Joseph was sold to Potiphar, one of the king's officers who was captain of the palace guard. In Potiphar's house, Joseph was put in charge of everything, since the Lord was with him and blessed him in everything he did. However, because he was a fine-looking young man, Potiphar's wife wanted to go to bed with him. No matter how hard she tried, Joseph refused. Finally one day she grabbed Joseph by his robe and tried to force him into bed. Joseph pulled away, leaving his robe in her hand. Then Potiphar's wife accused Joseph of rape so that he ended up in jail due to his master's fury for a crime he did not commit (Gen. 39).

Do not let your boss use you. Don't let that fine-looking lady trick you into going to bed with her; she will destroy you! Do not be attracted by those legs. They spell trouble! Do not let that man trick you by using his power and possessions! Stay faithful to the Lord, and run away from that hunky man!

Joseph told the truth to his master's wife, but he was thrown in jail. The Son of Man would be detained and would be convicted for reproving the world of wickedness. However, even in jail the jailer was pleased with Joseph and he was given responsibilities and put in charge. If we fear and obey the Lord, it does not matter if people reject us. Fear not men who have power to destroy and kill the flesh but not the spirit, rather fear God who has power to destroy both flesh and spirit (see Luke 12: 4–5). Wherever you go, the Lord will bless, and people who hate you will never kill your talent; it will blossom even under circumstances meant for its suppression.

The Lord used the route through jail to bring Joseph to his power. After interpreting the king's dreams, Joseph was made governor over Egypt. Following His crucifixion; Jesus was raised to the right hand of the Father and made the King over all. Everything that Joseph had dreamed at his young age came true, and his interpretation of dreams turned out just as he had said. During the famine, his father and brothers ended up bowing to him.

During the time when Joseph was in prison, the king of Egypt was offended by his wine steward and baker. He imprisoned the two men where Joseph was held prisoner. While in jail, the two men had dreams with different meanings, and Joseph interpreted them. The wine steward's dream meant that he would be restored to his position, and Joseph asked him to remember him once out of prison. The baker's dream meant that he would be executed. This series of events in a sense foretold that the Son of Man would be imprisoned and convicted with two sinners for a crime He did not commit. One of the sinners would be spiritually set free in heaven, while the other would be cast out to hell.

In the story of Joseph we learn a lot about doing well to those who wrong us. Later Joseph forgave his brothers and told them that what had happened between them was all orchestrated by God. Jacob's whole family moved to Egypt, where they were treated with respect and given land.

Before his death, Jacob called all his sons to give them blessings. In his blessings, Jacob prophesied what would become of each of the twelve tribes of Israel. However, here I will only mention the prophecy as it pertained to Judah. Jacob said that Judah would hold a sceptre and that nations would bow to him. It is interesting that the birth of the Saviour, who would become the King of kings and be praised throughout the world, was predicted so early! The Messiah came from the tribe of Judah as a descendant of David.

At this point I would like to invite you to a short prayer before we leave the beginnings and embark on the journey of life. It is indeed a good thing to prepare and have a good beginning before setting out on a journey, for we may not know the impediments that lie ahead.

> Oh Lord, You know all my troubles and needs. Every event is listed in Your diary. As I call to You in faith, my enemies will be turned back. I know, God, You are always on my side—the Lord whose promises never fail! In You I trust, and I choose faith over fear! What can a mere human do to me when I have You? Lord, may I daily walk in Your presence in the light that was in the beginning and forever shines on the living! Amen.

The Journey

Chapter 2

All journeys proceed from a defined location to a given destination. Journeys differ in length and the conditions that may be encountered along the way. Journeys also have a well-defined mission. They may serve business, leisure, exploration, or other purposes.

Life is also a journey that starts before an individual's birth and ends with a destination in the immortal and spiritual world. Before birth, there is a gestation period that defines and shapes our form so that we are ready to live on the world after birth. Following birth, there is also a spiritual process that prepares us for life after death as our bodies undergo changes in form, shaped by different circumstances they encounter.

There are many journeys we take in life. One of the most outstanding is the journey of the people of Israel as a nation starting in Egypt to the land promised to their predecessors. This journey portrays important spiritual messages of abiding, trust, love, faith, discipline, and endurance.

The generation of Joseph and his brothers died in Egypt, but their descendants, the Israelites, multiplied to become numerous. The Lord had kept His promise to His servants Abraham, Isaac, and Jacob that He would give them many descendants. From this journey we learn an important message: that through the journey of life, the Lord promises that He will look after us as long as we keep doing the right things and remaining faithful to His statutes. Even those who come against us may not conquer, for the power of the Lord is with us. He is the One who does not forget His promises.

Before any journey begins, an itinerary is prepared, and provisions are also arranged that will sustain those who are to embark on the trip. Before departing from the land of Egypt, the Israelites had to undergo serious hardships in slavery. They were made to do forced labour under strict regulations. When the ruler of Egypt saw that they were prospering despite their harsh living conditions, he commanded that their newborn baby boys should be brutally killed. All that happened to them was purposeful and significant towards the journey they would take out of the foreign land. These laborious and abominable deeds performed against them were meant to write an unforgettable history that would keep them from thirsting to return to the land of Egypt. It is also worth noting that their liberator was born at this excruciating time when a dark cloud covered their daily lives. It is therefore important to record that every time when the forces of evil seem to be operating at their peak in our lives, we should remember that the Lord is not asleep and that our liberation is at its final stages, as the darkest hour comes before dawn.

As a boy I used to enjoy hunting with older hunters and our pack of dogs. Sometimes we would set off on the journey as early as five o'clock in the morning. It was not rare that we would see days when until one o'clock in the afternoon we would not have come across a single animal! During this time one would normally be hungry and tired. We would therefore be dragging our legs on the way home when all of a sudden a wild animal would rise in our midst and make a sprint.

From this I learned an important lesson, that victory in life's journeys comes when we are about to give up! So focus, be well organized, keep those dreams alive, and dwell on the power of the Creator to bring them to pass. If an opportunity comes around when we have given up hope, we may fail to see it or lack the necessary enthusiasm to grab it, dragging our feet until it passes. Now through the birth of Moses, Israel was presented with a golden chance to escape their long-term oppression in Egypt.

At the time of Moses' birth, over a thousand years before the birth of our Lord, the descendants of Joseph and Jacob had lived in Egypt for some four centuries. Shortly before Moses was born, Egypt's pharaoh, by then ruler of a large empire extending over most of Canaan and Syria, decided to move his capital north to the delta region, where he could more effectively control his foreign subjects. There Pharaoh Seti I and his successor, the pharaoh of the Exodus, launched an ambitious building program. Using enormous numbers of slave labourers, they set about on a number of projects to rebuild old cities and construct new ones.

Daily, from dawn to dusk, Moses' father and other slaves toiled to make bricks for building huge buildings, walls, granaries, gates, and temples for the pharaoh. It was arduous work under the blazing Egyptian sun. Some of the men mixed mud with water, sand, and chopped straw. Others tramped upon the mixture for long hours with their bare feet, breaking it occasionally with wooden mattocks. When the muck was thoroughly blended, another group of slaves put it into wooden moulds to form bricks. The formed bricks were left to dry under the sun. This process was repetitive supervised by unsympathetic Egyptian overseers, ready to flog or savagely beat any stubborn slave even to death.

Despite these difficulties, the Israelite population continued to flourish. This demonstrates that the world may present us with all types of difficulties, hunger, insults, hatred, death of our beloved, and so on, but if the Lord is on our side, success will follow us in spite of the circumstances. Although pharaoh wanted to hamper the population growth of the Israelites by subjecting them to extremely hard work and throwing their newborn sons into the Nile, the Lord provided an ingenious plan whereby Moses' mother was able to hide him from the pharaoh's officials for three months without being discovered. On realizing that she could not conceal him for long, Moses' mother made a plan to save him. She wove a basket, set her son in it, and placed it among the reeds along the Nile. Miriam, the baby's sister, hid in the reeds, watching to see if her brother would be rescued.

The Bible (Exodus 2: 5–10) says that as the daughter of Pharaoh came to bathe at the river, she saw the basket among the reeds and sent her maid to fetch it. When she opened the basket, she found a baby crying. She recognized him as one of the Hebrew children and took pity on him. From this, it becomes clear that even amidst the most difficult times, the Lord will always watch over His chosen servants. Let me challenge you that as long as you were given a chance to be born into this world, you are an important messenger of the Lord, and He has a special plan for your life despite the hardships you may come across! He may send people to have pity on you even from amongst your foes!

Does your life feel as if you are trapped in a basket amongst reeds? Are you clouded by all sorts of problems, and it seems no one sees you? Relax! The Creator of the universe is sending someone to look over you and make sure you are rescued! The basket within which you are caged will soon be opened. You still have a lot of work ahead of you that the Lord has sent you to do! But take note that there still are expanses of barren desert to traverse in your journey.

Miriam witnessed the scene, came forward, and offered to find a Hebrew woman to nurture the child. When the pharaoh's daughter agreed, Miriam arranged for her own mother to care for the child. Until he was about three years old, Moses lived with his parents, sister, and older brother, Aaron, in what one would imagine must have been a poor family cabin or tent.

As he grew up, Moses gradually became acquainted with the world around him. He saw a world where men, women, and children laboured long hours with little time or energy for merriment. When he was three years old, he was returned to the pharaoh's daughter, who adopted him as her own son as per the initial agreement. Moses' life was a complete turnaround. He was given an Egyptian name, Moses, and raised as a prince in the palace. At about six years of age, he was sent to the temple school to be educated. He then began to wear the fine white linen loincloth and girdle of an Egyptian nobleman. At school, seated cross-legged on the floor, Moses and his mates learned to draw picture symbols on small, thin limestone under guidance of a temple scribe. Once they had mastered the hieroglyphic symbols and memorized passages from Egypt's classical writings, their work could be transferred onto scrolls of papyrus.

The story of Moses shows that he grew up to be a clever, handsome young man. By appearance he physically resembled an Egyptian nobleman. He was clean-shaven and scented with expensive oils and perfumes while wearing the fine white linen tunic and jewelled collar of a royal prince, as evident from some ancient Egyptian pictures. In Pharaoh's palace, Moses had quickly learned and mastered the skills of war, hunting, athletics, and leadership—all of which would become handy in his journey of life as dictated by the environment of his day. His weaknesses were few: a want of eloquence and the genetic inheritance and temperament of a hard-core Hebrew.

One day when Moses was walking past a construction site, he witnessed an Egyptian overseer brutally beating a tired Hebrew slave. Angered by such unkindness, Moses looked around to make sure no one saw him. He then attacked and beat the Egyptian to death. He buried the body in the sand and ran away. When Moses discovered that someone had seen him kill the Egyptian, he fled Egypt to take refuge in the Sinai Peninsula—a region which was nothing like the life he had encountered in the royal house of the pharaoh. There he had learned nobility and leadership, with the associated myth that those who rank high in society should be served. He seriously lacked outdoor survival skills.

Sometimes we go to school and get various certificates and think we know enough to get us through life. Others have roamed the streets and been through various hard situations, and they think they are well equipped and know the world. However, to walk through the journey of life and be prosperous, we must be multiskilled, focussed, and determined and know our purpose as set out by the Lord.

According to ancient history, the rugged, harsh land of the Sinai Peninsula harboured many foreigners looking for copper and turquoise. Hence, here Moses could quickly lose his Egyptian identity in the midst of the various groups of Asiatic slaves working mines for the Egyptians. As a result, concealed under these conditions, he would be hard to find.

The journey across barren Sinai must have been demanding for a man used to the lush delta region of Egypt. He was scorched in the baking desert sun as he hiked through the rough, all but lifeless country. He spent long days and nights without food and or water between the rare safe havens where he could find something to eat or drink. It was a desolate and hostile land dominated by steep, rusty mountains rising in serrated cliffs from the flat desert base.

In our lives we are confronted by assorted challenges. Many people have gone through various levels of education. Some have got a certificate or a degree; some have more than one degree. However, there are those who still cannot secure a good job or even become self-employed. The reality may be that the qualifications they hold are not compatible with the demands of life in their particular environment. Their upbringing may also be a strong factor in how they deal with the challenges confronting them in today's continuously changing world. Moses, with his Egyptian upbringing and royal education, had to learn new ways of survival in the forbidding Sinai Peninsula where there were no readily available meals. For him to eat, he had to quickly learn to find food in these foreign environs.

In the barren land Moses now had to live in, an occasional cluster of prickly scrub or a solitary acacia tree were the only signs of flora. The habitual schedule of Egyptian farming, controlled by the assurance of the Nile's annual floodwaters, was impossible in Sinai. Here precipitation was governed by sudden cloudbursts which came in winter and seeped rapidly into the sandy soil. Life here was precarious. It was a regular effort in antagonism to a hostile and erratic environment. In life we sometimes go through testing situations when we move out of our so-called comfort zone. It should be clear that if we are to go through the journey, we must be strong at heart and be of good faith with willingness to learn. We have to understand that we are constantly shaped by failures and adversities that time brings to our present. How we emerge out of all these determines the direction and progress of our journey.

In the land of Midian, the Bible says (Exodus 2: 16–21), Moses was sitting by a well, tired and hungry, as he wondered how he could survive in the foreign land. He realized that the schooling and skills he had acquired in Egypt were useless here. His predicament was solved when he met a group of Midianites. The Midianite people from southern Arabia had learned how to survive in this land. As Moses sat at the well, the daughters of Jethro came to water their father's flock of sheep. Before they had finished watering the animals, a group of shepherds came and drove the sheep from the well. Moses rescued the girls and then helped them finish watering the flock. When the girls reported the incident to their father, he asked them to call Moses so that he could eat bread with them. Moses agreed to the invitation and soon lived in Jethro's house afterwards. An important lesson here is that it is through giving to others that our lives may be made better. The good we do unto others becomes the good unto our own lives. In the course of our shared journey, we help each other across many bridges.

Moses married Jethro's daughter Zipporah, who bore him two sons, Gershom and Eliezer. In Midian Moses practically went through a new school under the mentorship of his father-in-law. He learned to care for flocks and was sent on journeys to find pastureland. He became accustomed to living in his new surroundings. He learned valuable skills such as finding water and food in unlikely places. He adapted and fit into the setting in Sinai.

Here the Lord, who had an important plan for Moses, wanted to complete a crucial training for a man He would send to liberate His people. The Lord wanted to equip Moses with tools that would become handy later in his leadership. Sometimes we become agitated and confused when life deals us a bad hand. The truth is that the Lord has other plans for our lives, and He has vital missions to send us on. Unless we are well trained with necessary skills, we might fail to fulfil His intended future missions. For this reason, it is important to fail early and learn crucial lessons.

If Moses had not fled Egypt, (moved out of his comfort zone), he could not have married Zipporah, and his two sons could have not been born to him. He could have missed learning the crucial survival skills to augment his Egyptian schooling. Many of us would not be where we are today if our lives had not been subjected to unyielding situations in our past. Some look back today and say: "It was painful. I never thought I would be able to forget it. I remember going through sleepless nights and spending days and nights in unbearable pain. I remember days in hostile situations, in fear and without a meal. But without those times, I could not be the person I am now. The circumstances have moulded me into what I am today. Am I truly driving this beautiful car today?"

It is important to note that although this was a necessary learning curve for Moses; to him it was an extremely difficult and sour life. It was not as easy as some of today's preachers might portray it. Moses experienced a life-threatening situation. There must have been times during the struggle for life in the desert when he pondered on questions like these: "Why was I born into this lonely and dangerous world? Why did I ever have to go through the Egyptian education which has become useless to my life today? Where is the God of my forefathers, Abraham, Isaac, and Jacob? Does He even exist? Will a day come in life when I will be out of this predicament, or am I going to die here?"

Don't these questions sound familiar to you? Often when we go through testing times in life, our minds are clouded by such questions. The reality is that those who have not gone through the same difficulties will never understand, for they have not been put to such a life-threatening test! When someone has lost loved ones, we usually try and console them and say that it will be okay. I am not saying that we should not pass along words of comfort, but the pain they suffer only becomes evident and practical the day we ourselves go through a similar situation.

A song like this one might have kept the lone fugitive thriving under the trying conditions of the unforgiving Sinai wilderness:

> In the course of all the troubles and trials I encounter, and the thorns that relentlessly prick the bottoms of my feet, I am kept going by the fact that the Lord always thinks of me! The troubles of life quickly overwhelm, upon my mind and soul their mistiness cast. Their shade is a constant reminder to my heart – The hairs on my body are counted! Let frosts fall, and let them thaw; let life shine, or be dark with misery. I am absolutely pleased; for I know for certain

that I am worth more than many sparrows! (This echoes the saying in Matthew 6: 25-34 in many English versions)

The Bible says that one day Moses was tending the flock of his father-in-law, Jethro, the priest of Midian. He let the flock wander far into the wilderness and came to Horeb in Sinai, the mountain of the Lord. There the angel of the Lord appeared to him in a blazing fire from the middle of a bush. Moses stared in amazement as the bush was engulfed in flames but was not consumed. Moses, asking himself why the bush was not burning up, came nearer. When the Lord saw that Moses wanted to take a close look, He called to him from the middle of the bush, "Moses! Moses!" Moses replied that there he was. "Do not come any closer," the Lord warned. "Take off your sandals, for you are standing on holy ground. I am the God of your ancestors, the God of Abraham, Isaac, and Jacob" (see Exodus 3: 3–6, TEV). Moses covered his face, for he was afraid to look at the Lord.

The Sinai region was barren and lonely. Nevertheless, it is amazing that the Lord did not appear to Moses when he was in the green Nile delta in Egypt, when he was enjoying princely status under Pharaoh's roof. Instead, the Lord revealed Himself under very difficult circumstances. Moses never had thought that it would be possible to meet the God of his forefathers in such an unlikely place—not when he was a fugitive with the crime of murder lingering over his soul.

Let me appeal to you if you feel as though you are at your darkest hour now. It seems you are in a nonproductive place and state of your life, and you may even think that the Lord has forgotten you. Please get up and say: "Lord, I know You are with me now although I may not see You. I know You have seen every wrongdoing against Your servant, and I know this is Your chance to reveal Yourself when things seem darkest, for You want me to grow in faith and leadership."

Please note that sometimes, when we are covered in the riches of this world and everything seems to be going all right, we may not become spiritually cautious and mature, and we may not even listen to our Lord even as He is revealing Himself to us. The reality is that people do not need anything to rely on as long as they think nothing is threatening their lives, and therefore their determination and efforts may die. Today you may have lost your loved one, you may be in an abusive relationship, you may have lost your job, your child may have been raped, or it may seem as if you are in a desert where the only sign of life is a thorny shrub. Remember, it is time for the Lord to reveal Himself!

It is interesting to realize what the Lord said to Moses. The Lord had certainly seen the subjugation of His people in Egypt. He had heard the sobs of sorrow because of their ruthless slavedrivers. Yes, He was aware of their misery. So He had come down to liberate them from the supremacy of the Egyptians and escort them out of Egypt into their own large, abundant land, a land flowing with milk and honey. Certainly the Lord is aware of the difficult life you lead—that you and your children do not have food, that your friends loved you when you were working, but ever since you lost your job, they have no use for you.

The Lord is sending His Moses to deliver you from your house of bondage. Not a single unfair treatment against you has escaped the Lord's sight. All your cries have reached His ears! Remember, He heard the cry of Ishmael from under the tree where his mother had left him to die. Get ready to escape those nasty conditions for the Promised Land, the land with the Lord's peace!

Moses thought that he was not fit to be sent on the liberation mission. So he questioned the Lord about his fitness to appear before the majesty of the pharaoh and his ability to show the Israelites the way out of Egypt. Does this sound familiar? Most of the time we doubt ourselves, with an eye to our physical appearance, our financial situation, our family lineage, and our educational status. The Lord our Father knows exactly what we are capable of. He knew us before He created us; He has a definite purpose for us and a vision of how He wants to use us. He confirmed that He would be with Moses and gave him a credible sign that, once he had liberated the people from Egypt, Moses would worship Him at that very mountain of Sinai.

Moses was protesting that he did not think it was possible to accomplish the mission that the Lord had sent him. On the other hand, God was absolutely sure that the journey would be a success, so that Moses and the people of Israel would worship Him on Horeb (commonly called Mount Sinai). Whenever we do something in the journey of life that will benefit others and glorify the Lord, we should learn to carry it out with all our might without looking back, since the Lord will support us in fulfilling the course He created us for.

The Lord told Moses that the king of Egypt would not let the Israelites go unless a mighty hand forced him. So the Lord would raise His hand and strike the Egyptians, performing all kinds of miracles among them. Then at last Pharaoh would let the people of Israel go, and the Lord would cause the Egyptians to look favourably on the Israelites so that they would give them gifts when they left. Yes, when the Lord's designated time has come, even your enemies will do you favours. Your unkind boss at work will find it necessary to give an increase, treat you with respect, and even promote you. Your abusive husband will treat you with respect and love you as you deserve. Your negligent parents will look after you and support you as they should. The Lord has allowed you to go through all that trouble so that you may not forget where you came from when you are liberated.

Moses carried on protesting: "What if they won't believe me or listen to me? What if they say the Lord never appeared to me?" It is surprising how we normally worry about things that may crop up as we leap into taking a step in life and seizing an opportunity. Some of us are even scared that others might laugh at us. What if I take this chance and fail? What will people say? We never dwell much on what if we succeed! What if all that we worry about does not happen?—which is usually the case. We must learn to focus on the Lord and His might, with faith. If He created us and all that we see in the universe, then our challenges should easily come to His feet.

Following a number of plagues, at last Pharaoh agreed to let the Hebrews go. One may ask why it was necessary for the Lord to harden Pharaoh's heart. It was important for the Israelites to feel the pain so that they would always remember from one generation to another how their God—the God of their ancestors Abraham, Isaac, and Jacob—had delivered them from the house of bondage. The nature of human beings is such that they forget quickly what they were, once life conditions are favourable. In today's world, we meet many jobless people. It often happens that these people, once they have secured a job, do not adhere to the rules and conditions at their jobs. They grow defiant and full of protests. At the time when they asked to be hired, they were humble and obedient. Likewise, when a man or woman requires a partner, they are humble and begging, but after securing what they want, they become stubborn and uncaring.

The final plague wrought in Egypt was that in which the Lord killed the eldest sons of the Egyptians. To protect the Hebrew families from this plague, the Lord had ordered Moses to tell them to prepare a special meal. Each family was to kill an unblemished one-year-old male lamb in the evening. The families were to roast and eat all the meat that same night, with bitter herbs and unleavened bread. Some of the lamb's blood was to be collected during slaughtering. Then the head of each household was to daub the doorposts on top and on either side with a bunch of hyssop dipped in the lamb's blood. When the Lord came to the house marked with blood, He would "pass over," leaving its occupants safe.

It is wise to daub our doorposts with the branch of hyssop dipped in the Lamb's blood. When the Lord visits us, He will identify us as His and keep our houses safe. He will also bless us. We can do this by keeping our ways clean and worshiping, by not losing hope, and by staying determined. Those who always set their minds on the Lord and abide by His laws are like people who have daubed their doorposts with the lamb's blood. Wherever they go, blessings will follow them, for they bear the sign of the Lord their Father. Today we have the new Lamb, the Messiah, the Son of Man. Believing in Him and following His teaching is like daubing our doorposts with the lamb's blood as the Israelites did preceding their liberation in Egypt.

When the Israelites were finally released from Egypt, the Lord did not lead them along the shortest route that runs through Philistine territory. The Lord said, "If the people are faced with battle, they might change their minds and return to Egypt." So the people were taken in a roundabout way through the wilderness towards the Red Sea. The caravan left Succoth and camped at the edge of the wilderness at Etham. The Lord led and guided them during the day with a pillar of cloud and a pillar of fire by night. This allowed the journey to continue by day and night.

Note that it was purposeful that the people were not taken through the shortest route. This helped them to harden and learn important lessons. It is amazing how in our lives we always want to take the shortest routes in doing things. Sometimes when starting a new business we want everything to quickly gel up. Any project that reaches its climax without a solid foundation is bound to collapse. This is because it has not gone through the necessary testing times to obtain strength for the long haul. That is why some individuals who win a lottery and suddenly find themselves rich overnight soon find themselves in trouble. Some important sustainability pillars should be in place to support any success journey. Even in the army, someone who has just joined may not be made a general. Instead, someone who has gone through years of hard training and is well conversant with the strategies of the army is made into a general. Such people have gained valuable training and experience and should stand the test of time.

When we go through the struggles of life to get what we want, it may seem we are taking a roundabout way. Sometimes we may despair, and yet this is how we are shaped to be able to persist on the journey of success. When we face difficulties in whatever we do, or when life deals us a bad hand, let us remember that the Lord is still ahead of us with a pillar of cloud by day and a pillar of fire by night. We are told in Numbers 9: 15–23 that the Israelites set up and broke camp according to the commands given by the Lord through Moses. Their movement was controlled by the movement of the cloud that rested upon the Tent of the Lord. Therefore, if things seem stagnant in our lives now, it is because the cloud has not moved, and therefore we may not break camp. It is important to note that if we go on and do things by ourselves, we will have broken camp without command. Then we will be leaving the Lord behind and acting out of our own will. Our journey ahead becomes fatal, for we do not know the Promised Land or how to enter it; nor do we know the correct route to follow. Then if the Lord is for us and leads us, who dares be against us? Who can be a better leader than the Creator of all things and the one who knows everyone's purpose in life?

Then the Lord instructed Moses to order the Israelites to turn back and camp by Pi-Hahiroth between Migdol and the sea. They were to camp along the shore, across from Baal-Zephon. Then Pharaoh would think that the Israelites were confused. Pharaoh would think that they were trapped in the wilderness. Once again the Lord would harden Pharaoh's heart, and he would chase after Moses and the Israelites. The Lord had planned this in order to display His glory through Pharaoh and his whole army. After this the Egyptians would know that the Lord was God. So the Israelites did as they were told.

It often happens in our journeys of life that when it seems things are going smoothly, we come across hiccups that seem to slow our success voyage and even take us backwards. There are people who have held high positions in high-paying jobs, but today their lives are stagnant and burdened with debts. For others there were times when business was flourishing, but today things have slowed down. In relationships, once love was burning, but it is a bit sluggish today. Relax! You have just been ordered to turn back and camp by Pi-Hahiroth; there is a good reason for this if you trust in the Lord! You will soon be smiling as the Lord unveils His plan. After that, you and your enemies will both know that Jehovah is the Lord!

On hearing that the Israelites had fled, Pharaoh and his officials changed their minds and decided to pursue them. They took 600 of Egypt's best chariots with their commanders. Pharaoh and his troops chased after the Israelites and caught up with them beside the shore near Pi-Hahiroth, across from Baal-Zephon.

The people of Israel panicked when they saw the Egyptians overtake them. They cried out to the Lord and pelted Moses with questions: "You, man, tell us why you brought us out here to die in the wilderness? Was there not enough land for our graves in the land of Egypt? Look at what you have done to us! Why did you convince us to leave Egypt? Didn't we tell you while we were still in Egypt that exactly this would happen? We told you to leave us alone! We told you to let us be slaves to the Egyptians. It would have been better for us to be slaves in Egypt than to become corpses in the wilderness!"

Moses calmed the people and told them not to be afraid. He told them to just stand still and watch the Lord rescue them. He reassured them that the Egyptians they saw would never be seen again. The Lord himself would fight for Israel.

Just stay calm. Let me challenge you now! Don't be afraid! Just stand still, and watch the Lord rescue you from those rapists, gangsters, drugs, and a myriad of iniquities that want to own you! They may seem to have overtaken you, but it is only to their detriment.

In times of hardship our minds run wild; we shake in fear at situations that threaten to take our lives. All hope is gone, and we think it must be the end of us. Things are not going well and we think, "Why did I take this chance? Now everybody is going to laugh at me. I have made a complete fool of myself! My friends who were not even clever at school are overtaking me, and things seem to be going smoothly for them." Stay calm and watch the Lord rescue you today! Just stay calm; the Lord himself will fight for you! You have done everything you could; the circumstances seem beyond your powers; you are deep in debt, you don't see how you are going to pay those school fees, and they are about to take your house and repossess your car. Please stay calm and watch the Lord rescue you today! You are in pain, groaning in that hospital bed at home; you think it is over with your life because normally history shows that, with your kind of illness, people die. Please stay calm, determined, and focussed. Remember, you are camped by Pi-Hahiroth, across from Baal-Zephon, and you are awaiting the Lord's miracle so that you may know that He alone is the Lord. You are taken care of, watched over by a pillar of cloud by day and a pillar of fire by night.

When the Lord heard the Israelites crying out to Him in fear, He commanded Moses to tell the people to get moving. He told Moses to pick up his staff and raise his hand over the sea. Moses was commanded to divide the water so that the people could walk on dry ground through the sea. Then the Lord sent a strong east wind to drive back the sea, and the waters were divided to form a wall on both sides. The Israelites crossed on dry land with the waters of the sea towering on their left and right. All Pharaoh's charioteers and horsemen went after them into the sea in pursuit. When all the

Israelites had made it across, Moses was commanded to raise his hand over the sea again. The water rushed back to its original place covering and killing all Egyptians, without one of them surviving. Yes! None of your troubles will remain after the Lord has taken care of them! Halleluiah! When Moses and the people saw what the Lord had done to the Egyptians, they sang: "I will sing to the Lord, because He has won a glorious victory; ... You, Lord, will be king forever and ever!" (see Exodus 15: 1–18, TEV).

Because we do not see the Lord with our eyes, it may seem He doesn't even exist during times of trouble. Sometimes our troubles weigh heavily on us and elicit panic. Our minds run wild, calculating and jumping to conclusions about how dangerous the situation looks and how it may all end up. Let us remember that the Lord puts us through certain situations so that His glory may be witnessed. If we believe that we are His children and do what is righteous, there is no single situation He may use against us. Let the charioteers of poverty and hunger, those of insults hurled by your enemies, the pain caused by the loss of your loved ones, the pain and remorse caused by all life's circumstances—let it all be swallowed by the sea at the Lord's command. You entered the sea with fear and trembling. You must emerge on the opposite shore a winner, with your burdens swallowed by prayer and the power of the Lord.

The challenges in the journey of life are many, and they follow us along the way. One after the other, they strengthen us spiritually and shape us for our destination (the Promised Land). The escape to Sinai through the Red Sea was only the beginning of an onerous journey. Moses and his people still faced trying times ahead. This is why it was important for Moses to have earlier gone through the barren desert so he could learn important leadership skills. Otherwise he would be helpless and fail to lead his people, who would be looking up to him at this difficult time. Since he had been there before, his calm became a ray of hope in the eyes of his people, even though they sometimes lost control. The situation would have worse if he had to cry with them whenever they cried in fear.

From the Red Sea Moses let the people out into the wilderness of Shur, where they travelled for three days without finding water. When they came to the oasis of Marah, the water was bitter and undrinkable. Then the people cried out to Moses for a drink. For days the caravan had trudged through the parched expanses that almost seemed endless. After consulting with the Lord, Moses easily remedied the situation. He took a tamarisk tree and threw it into the water, which subsequently became sweet. Both the people and their livestock drank and took some for the journey. The caravan headed to the oasis of Elim where they found twelve springs, wearily pitched their tents, and camped for several weeks.

Although we may share the same present moment in time, we are undergoing different challenges. Some have gone for days without a meal while others have their plates overflowing. Some are crying while others are laughing their lungs out. Some are sick and in pain while others are well and healthy. Some have welcomed a newborn while others are grieving the loss of a child. All these bitter situations will be remedied. The waters will be sweet upon throwing a tamarisk—the Lord's Word and prayer. Sometimes the journey comes to very steep ascent, after which a rest is needed for replenishment and recuperation.

Refreshed by their camp at Elim, the contingent traversed the Wilderness of Sin towards the Sinai Mountains and Mount Horeb, where Moses had first met the Lord and would return to pray and make a covenant. After a few days, the people began to complain again. It was now one month after they had left the land of Egypt. They growled and grumbled about how they used to have plenty of vegetables and bread and sit next to pots of meat in Egypt. They told Moses that he had brought them out of Egypt to kill them with hunger in the desert. Angered by the complaints of the people, Moses called them together and rebuked them for their lack of faith in the Lord.

Often people want to see quick results and quick returns. This became very clear when I worked with communities on environmental conservation projects. It was not easy to get their concurrence as the communities wanted to see quick benefits. Since we cannot look into the future and see what is coming, we become shaky and agitated when things do not go our way or we do not get what we want when we want it. If only we could see what the Lord has planned and what time is bringing towards us. Unfortunately, what the future brings along is only known to the Lord, and ours is to keep hope and faith.

According to Moses' promise, the Lord demonstrated His power by bringing food to the hungry Israelites. In the evening vast numbers of quail flew in and covered the camp. The next morning dew lay around the camp and when it evaporated, a flaky substance had covered the face of the wilderness. It tasted like honey, and Israel called it manna. Their hunger satisfied and their faith momentarily restored, the Israelites continued their journey across the wilderness of Sin.

Soon, however, a new challenge confronted them. At Rephidim they met with Amalekites who attacked them, most probably to stop the Israelites from occupying territory along their trade routes between Arabia and Egypt. The Israelites had never before been proven in battle, and they were not well equipped. They possessed simple weapons carried by shepherds to protect their flocks. They had slings, staffs, crude spears, and simple bows and arrows. On the other hand, the Amalekites were armed with bronze-tipped arrows, spears, and swords. Moses assembled an army of his strongest men, equipped them, and chose young, zealous Joshua to lead them into battle.

Moses, accompanied by Aaron and a man named Hur, climbed a nearby hill to watch his new army in battle. The Bible says whenever Moses held up his hand, Israel triumphed, and whenever he lowered his hand, Amalek overcame. As Moses' hands grew weary, Aaron and Hur sat him on a stone and held his hands high, one on either side. Joshua cut down Amalek and his people with the edge of the sword.

Following the war, there was great rejoicing in the Israelite camp. Moses built a rough stone altar on which he sacrificed a lamb for the Lord and he named it Yahweh-nissi ("the Lord is my banner") (Exodus 17: 8–16).

Shortly thereafter the caravan reached desert of Sinai, where the Israelites pitched their tents on a narrow plain at the foot of the tall granite mountain, Horeb. When we make a journey for the first time, we see new places and meet new challenges. When I was employed in conservation projects I was confronted with challenges I had never come across before. I remember when I was first promoted to Senior Conservation and Cultural Heritage Specialist. No one except my boss believed that I would make it. I was just like Joshua, chosen to lead a novice army into battle. However, to my surprise and to that of others, I did that job very well. The same fears and circumstances came when I was promoted to be a project coordinator and lead the whole multi-stakeholder bilateral project. With the hand of the Lord, the project ran smoothly, and we wrote a good Implementation Completion Report (ICR). I never prevailed by my own strength but because the mighty hand of the Lord was raised. I realized victory because of the one who sent me, for no slave is greater than his master!

Following renewal of their covenant with the Lord on Mount Sinai and building a sanctuary for Him, the Israelites left Sinai and headed northward toward Canaan. A new set of tests lay ahead. They packed their belongings and placed the sacred ark of the covenant on two long poles which the priests carried ahead of the caravan. They slowly trekked until they came to the wilderness of Paran after several weeks. In terms of its geomorphology, the wilderness of Paran is a hostile chalk and limestone plateau stretching some eighty miles along the eastern perimeter of the Sinai peninsula. Under this hostile environment, the Israelites were drained of faith again. They daily complained of hunger, with their hearts turning back and pining for their lost Egyptian life. At this time even their leader Moses became frustrated and began to question the Lord. He complained and asked why the Lord had treated him so badly and why the Lord had burdened him with responsibility for the people of Israel.

I often watch new couples getting married for the first time. The day of the wedding is overflowing with happiness, and it seems there will never be challenges in the relationship. However, down the line the couples experience difficulties that they must learn to overcome. Some look back and remember their other extra relationships they had before marriage. Some start regretting that they married the person they are with. They think things might have been different had they got married to somebody else.

The reality is that they have embarked on a journey. They need to accept that there will be stretches where they might not find water and food. They will come across some barren desert where they may not find a meal. At such times they should cling together and show the true colours of their love. Most important, they should remember that the Lord who watched them take their vows is going ahead of them in the covenant ark carried by their priests. They will soon be at Kadesh–Barnea.

Finally the Israelites reached the periphery of the wilderness and took rest at Kadesh–Barnea. Here they were only fifty miles from the southern margin of the Promised Land (Canaan). Moses sent twelve spies to investigate the land's people and its defences. Joshua, son of Nun, and Caleb were among the spies. Moses instructed them to be of good courage and to bring some of the fruit of the land. Some weeks later the men came back laden with grapes, figs, and pomegranates.

Then Moses summoned all the people to hear the news. The spies reported that they had come to a land flowing with milk and honey and displayed its fruits for the people. They also reported that the people of the land were strong and the cities, fortified and large; they had also encountered the descendants of Anak (a giant). When hearing the report, the people's hearts sank. They wondered why the Lord would take them this far to fall by the sword. Only Joshua and Caleb believed in the power of Israel to conquer Canaan. They urged that Israel had to go at once and conquer the land. However, the other spies insisted on how strong the people of the land were, saying they felt like grasshoppers in comparison to them. They cried out that they had to choose a captain and go back to Egypt.

I have often heard people complain: "The business I want to start needs a lot of capital. How on earth am I going to raise that amount of money? The government of this land is so corrupt and stubborn, how am I going to succeed? After all, I do not belong to the ruling party; I might as well give up! ... This marriage is not working. I remember the same thing happened with so-and-so, and they ended up in a divorce. Things are not looking good—this illness is too strong, and they say people never survive." All sorts of thoughts come to our minds to discourage us. If we are not of good faith, we are soon swept by the emotional river into the gutter.

Joshua and Caleb tried to calm the people down. Yet it was to no avail, for the angry mob decided to stone them. Suddenly they stopped as the glory of the Lord appeared to everybody at the tent of the meeting. The Lord asked Moses how long the people would despise Him after all the miracles He had performed amongst them.

Moses pleaded for forgiveness, but unfortunately this time the Lord was not to forgive so easily. The Lord instructed Moses to tell the people that, as surely as He lived, what the people of Israel had said in His hearing He would do to them. Their dead bodies would fall in the wilderness. Thus the Israelites were condemned to wander in the wilderness of Sinai for a generation. The generation who had come out of Egypt would never set foot in the Promised Land.

Shocked by the harsh punishment, many refused to accept as true that they would never enter Canaan after coming so far. In fact, a few organized themselves into an armed group and tried to invade Canaan from the south, but they were turned back by a collaborative effort of Canaanites and Amalekites. It took many years before Israel's morale was vigorous enough to invade Canaan successfully.

The same thing happens in our lives. Once time presents some difficulties, some of us begin to think that the Lord isn't there. We start complaining and irritating our heavenly Father: "Why is this happening to me? I cannot afford to live this way! I am as good as dead!" All these complaints are characteristic of a person who has lost hope and faith. We have to be careful about whining and remember that the Lord is listening, lest we are condemned to wander without going straight to our intended destination—whether it is building that house, buying that car, or getting that college qualification, that tender, or that promotion.

Because of the condemnation, Moses and his people camped and pastured their animals near Kadesh-Barnea for a generation. The older generation of those who had left Egypt died out, being replaced by strong younger people who were prepared to follow the Lord's commands. This generation was raised from infancy with the Lord's laws and commandments. They eagerly longed for the day when they would enter the Promised Land at the Lord's command. It is important to note that the hearts of these young men and women were fixed on their God. They believed they could not do anything without Him, and they wanted Him to lead them.

It was unfortunate that even Moses would not enter the Promised Land. Towards the end of their camp in Kadesh-Barnea, his faith in the Lord had faltered. One day his people had run out of water, and Moses had asked the Lord for help. The Lord had commanded Moses and his brother Aaron to take his rod and assemble the crowd and to tell the rock before their eyes to yield its water.

Moses and Aaron gathered the people. Moses rebuked the people and instead of doing as the Lord had commanded, he lifted up his hand and struck the rock twice with his rod although he was to speak a command. Water gushed out of the rock. The people and their animals drank. But this act infuriated the Lord so that He decided not to permit Moses and Aaron to bring the congregation into the land which He had given them.

Although it must have been a nightmare for Moses to be punished so severely, he accepted his fate without question and understood that to him time had brought the end. With a sunken heart he assembled his people and began the last lap of his extensive expedition. He would lead the Israelites to the border of Canaan and there for evermore depart from them. This time the Israelites marched to the Gulf of Aqaba and joined the King's Highway, an old caravan route in eastern Canaan. The plan was to go through the kingdoms of Edom and Moab, cross the Jordan, and launch an attack from Canaan's more vulnerable eastern border.

The hope of travelling through Edom was abandoned when the king of Edom refused to grant Moses and the Israelites permission to pass through his land. The king promised to attack them if they insisted, and he sent a band of soldiers to stop them from crossing. Moses avoided war and led his people up the trough of Araba along Edom's western border. On the southern border of Moab, Moses was again denied permission to enter the kingdom of Moab. The Israelites were forced to bypass Moab and go through the desolate wilderness to the east. Farther east stretched the Arabian desert.

At the northern border of Moab, the caravan finally turned westwards towards Canaan. Nevertheless, there was still a hitch in their path. Sihon, the king of the territory directly north of Moab, refused to let the people go through his land. Instead he sent soldiers to stop them. With no alternative, the Israelites were forced into battle at Jahaz. They overcame Sihon's army and carried on westward. Their way followed a gentle upward gradient across a limestone plateau. On ascending the elevated central ridge of the plateau, the procession laid eyes upon part of the meandering Jordan and the land of Canaan. They cried out in joy and approval, despite their exhaustion. Their voices skyrocketed in praise of the Lord. With invigorated spirit they descended to the plains of Moab where they would camp in preparation to launch the attack on Canaan.

Due to the punishment he had sustained, Moses could not fully partake in his people's euphoria. He knew that he had reached the climax of his tedious journey and that soon he would forever be taken away from these people. With a sad spirit and sunken heart he summoned his people to give them a final lecture. The young nation assembled at the feet of its beloved leader. The aged figure with white hair and wrinkled face and hands stood before them. The long years of wandering in hostile environments, the endless complaints, the disappointments, and the burden of responsibility—all had claimed their fair share of him. Only his eyes still glimmered with juvenile spirit, and certainty and vigour infused his words.

He steadily recounted for the congregation the tale of the Israelite escape from the house of bondage and their pilgrimage to Mount Sinai. Then he reiterated the words the Lord had spoken to him on the holy mountain and charged them to keep the commandments and the laws. If they fully obeyed the Lord through keeping His commandments, statutes, and ordinances, they would live to prosper in the land they were about to possess. Moses also declared to them that they would perish if drawn to foreign cults and worshiping of foreign gods.

Then Moses told his people who were listening attentively that he was a hundred and twenty years old. He told them that he was no longer able to go out and come in and that the Lord had told him that he would never go over the Jordan. The Lord their God Himself would go over ahead of the Israelites, and Joshua would lead them as the Lord had spoken. Moses told them to be strong and to be of good courage and not to fear, for it was the Lord who went with them, and He would not fail or forsake them.

His message delivered, Moses picked up his shepherd's staff and left. He walked alone across the plain to the base of Mount Nebo. The old man slowly climbed up the steep rocky mass and finally reached the apex. From the summit he could see his people camped far below on the plain. As the sun had begun to descend beyond the horizon, he saw flickering fires among the tents. His eyes finally came to rest upon the sacred tabernacle which stood venerated at the centre of the large square encampment. Smoke issued in black clouds from a sacrificial altar where the Levites were sacrificing a lamb.

He unwillingly turned and gazed westward over the far side of the mountain. There in the rays of the setting sun lay the land of Canaan. He admired the fertile green valley of the Jordan below, beyond which lay the Canaanite city of Jericho. To the south, the waters of the Dead Sea glimmered red and gold in the sunset, and the purple Judean hills rose sharply westward towards Jerusalem. His eyes devoured the twisting course of the Jordan northward to the blue waters of Lake Galilee and the rough, rocky hills of central

Canaan westward. This view encompassed the land that was soon to be occupied by the juvenile generation of Israel.

This scenery occupied Moses' eyes for a long time until the blanket of dusk completely engulfed the land as the sun sank out of sight. Then Moses closed his eyes, and with the portrait of the Promised Land incised in his mind and soul, the great man died. Now Joshua was faced with the daunting task of leading his people over the Jordan. He would meet challenges—above all, "This man is not like Moses. Moses did not do this and that. We would have been happy under Moses." These sorts of complaints are not new to those who have been promoted to take over leadership at their organizations.

This was the journey of Moses and his people, but it shows us that we should not give up our hope and faith, no matter how difficult the circumstances that confront us may be. It is important to listen and act in obedience at the Lord's appointed time. I have heard a story from a man who has climbed Mount Everest. He told me that it is important to have reached a certain point along the climb at a certain time of day. If a climber has not made it to this point at the particular time, it is almost certain that he will not summit the mountain. Many have died and their remains have to date not been recovered from the slopes of Everest. The initial generation that left Egypt with Moses wasted a lot of time complaining about many things, and they lost focus on the Lord and the journey and as a result many left their flesh and bones to the barren desert. Likewise, in our lives a plethora of happenings may divert us from our focal point so that we end up losing the battle before coming to our intended destination.

Notice also, oh dear Theophilus, that the last trip Moses took to climb Mount Nebo was not an easy one! He had to overcome the rocky mass before he made it to the apex. The journey of our lives is no different. There are rocky masses to overcome before we make it to where we want to be. Whether it is in a social relationship or a business endeavour, in sports or various career pathways, our journey to success is confounded by various challenges before we make it to the summit where we may be able to look west, east, north, and south and be fulfilled by what our journey of success holds for us. Believe me, this will be the fraction of time at the brink of our pilgrimage to the next world!

Following the loss of my job I tried to venture into the transport business. The move made me lose all my savings and plunge into bankruptcy. Everything I tried was in vain. The situation kept worsening until I could not afford to pay school fees for my children, or put bread on the table for my family without help from my spiritual father and mother. In August 2004, I had lost my elder brother who was mysteriously shot and killed. In 2005 I lost my nephew to illness, and then on 19 January 2006 I lost my biological mother. In January 2007 I lost my grandmother (my father's mother). In 2011, in the midst of all trouble and pennilessness, I lost two daughters and a driver in a tragic car accident. Hence, I wrote:

The last words to Mathabo and Mantšanana

A myriad of questions cloud my mind, but there are no definite answers. As the war frontiers draw near and close on me, the heavens have gone silent for nature owes no one an explanation. Then I stumble feebly and fumble as I page through my Bible in search for weaponry and condolences. After reading through a number of gospels it suddenly dawned to me. I did not partake when the Creator created the universe. Neither am I part of the heavenly meetings that decide on the supernatural calendar of events. Today the universal belt of time has presented to my present a bitter strip.

Time throws events to men like a stormy ocean of frenzied waves. You were given unto us to perform a special function. Like the audience in a theatre we sat and watched in amusement as you performed. As the show was progressively heating up and we started to squirm on our seats in approval, you left the stage in a sudden blast of thunder and blinding light. We are left blind and bewildered, asking whither are they vanished? The last link we have with you is the eddy of dust spiralling from the stage and odour from your heated bodies.

Mathabo and Mantšanana! What leaders we have seen in such young people! Today it has dawned to me that I am nothing but dust settled from generations who thrived centuries before me. My flesh has been borrowed and will disintegrate into various components to join the cycles of nature. Only my spirit that came from the Creator will go back to Him and join the multitudes who have once roamed the face of our desolate world. The extent of loss felt by our sore hearts is immeasurable by physical and mechanical balnces. Your irreplaceability index would amount to unity in conservation scales—where species disappear from Mother Nature not ever to be recovered to occupy their ecological niches.

Lord, Thou wilt deliver! Lord, Thou wilt defend! In the course of all the troubles and trials I encounter, and the thorns that relentlessly prick the base of my feet, I am kept going by the fact that there is a universal power that always thinks of me! The troubles of life quickly overwhelm, upon my mind and soul their mistiness cast; their shade is a constant reminder to my heart—the hairs on my body are counted! Let frosts fall, and let them thaw, let life shine, or be dark with misery. I am absolutely pleased; for I know for real—I am worth more than many sparrows!

Goodbye, good roses! You will forever dwell in our minds and hearts. Our brains will ponder your memories to our dusty death! Your mortal lives were soon nibbled to oblivion as rats would to a morsel of cheese! Your portrait dangles from the dusty walls of my heart. It is etched to remain a legacy resembling the prolific rock art by the San who once wandered the gorges and plains of our land.

I battle to conserve my strength to come to terms with my loss. I have gone pale like a yellow crop displaying evidence that the field upon which it stands has given away nutrients through heavy leaching. The delectable landscapes upon which you once marched with joy have become agape and will soon swallow your remains. To us time has untimely snatched you away as hawks do to chickens. Our wingspan fell short that we could have leaped to your protection.

Water from the small puddles scattered above the sandstone plateaus has evaporated in the blazing heat of summer. A map work of cracks is laid on the sediment adorning their base where once upon a time tadpoles danced. New life will spring with the arrival of the eagerly awaited torrents. Our spiritual meadows will again flourish with lush green—following the blazes of wildfires that have once swept through the countryside. *Mesembryanthemums* and various other

flowers will once more garnish the plateaus that stand
as landmarks on our landscape.

Today I understand why I saw tears in my father's eyes sixteen years
ago. Although he did not cry with audible bitterness that choked his
throat, it was evident that the agony he felt emanated from a deeply
ravaged heart. It was during the loss of his daughter, my elder sister.
His grief could not be concealed, and his eyes were glazed with tears
that eventually rolled down on either side of his face, meandering
through his freshly cut beard.

I had found a note tucked under my dormitory door. It told me that
my sister at home had passed away. It was during the years when I
was at college. I came from one of those night laboratory sessions
at the institution where I was busy working towards my honours
degree. The next morning I had to take a taxi to travel more than
four hundred kilometres from school to my home.

Since I had found the note at midnight, I had no time to inform my
supervisor. He was a balding middle-aged man (may his soul rest in
peace). The remainder of his hair was always neatly cut short into
brush. Both his hair and stubble of beard contained an even mixture
of black and grey hairs. I would inform him later that I'd had to
unexpectedly rush home.

I arrived home at six o'clock in the evening. The whole family was
already assembled. I greeted them and sat down. After a cup of
coffee they began to relate the story of my sister's departure. This is
when I began to see tears roll down my father's cheeks. The event
made me feel weak in the joints and wonder if ever things would
resume normality. What an unforgettable scene! I guess even to
those without photographic memory such things would not require
an effort to recall.

Six months after my children had passed away, the family prepared a ceremony to unveil tombstones in their memory. Then in their memory I felt that I had to write:

Unveiling of Tombstones

It is not so long ago when the heaviest and fiercest of storms charged. The world of our hearts seemed torn beyond repairs. Lightning struck, leaving ditches all over the landscape and scars from boulders that frantically ran loose with sound echoing to stir unrest in valleys. The situation was disastrous. The gale winds knocked down even the toughest of trees so that they fell, crushing their branches while their roots were torn free from the medium of their anchorage. Our eyes were left sore from the dust blown in, and our chests whooping with cough. The rehabilitation processes have just begun.

The runoff left an assortment of gullies that will take a patient spiritual process to rehabilitate. The landscape of our hearts has incessantly been eroded to its bedrock. The most important of species have been lost to extinction, and they cannot be replaced. Come oh eagle of eternity, you who soars above the blue skies and dives deep down below the deepest seas. Blow the heavenly breath – the Holy Spirit, use time to reconstruct a new landscape of faith and hope. Use the heavenly gabions—the Scripture—to rehabilitate and retain the collapsing walls.

Nothing compares to the pain of losing one's child, except to those heartless ones who throw children in dust bins, abduct, rape, and kill them. Today's world has turned into butchery for our children; others are mutilated and their parts sold for money, while some are drug mules or even sold for sex. Let us come to our senses! Mathabo and Mantšanana, losing you has taught me that pain cannot be shared. Each man feels it according to the final interpretation given by their brains.

This day arouses mixed memories. I remember the time you began to talk. The first word you pronounced was dad (*ntate*). Memories bring back all the sweetest of times we spent, from the time you smeared yogurt all over your faces as toddlers to brilliant young women who demonstrated a lot of responsibility for your age. Indeed you were a jewel to our family. I do not want to regurgitate the time when I found you lying silent and dead beside the road, and I dread to replay the day of your post-mortem, for fear I will choke and collapse to death.

This day shakes and agitates the benthos of our hearts. From our heat-oppressed brains, memories rise spiralling like silt from the base of a tadpole-disturbed pool towards its surface leaving the waters turbid and their crystal clarity momentarily lost. We hastily flip through the archives in our brains; it is amazing how many deposits of you confront us. No doubt with time we shall heal, but we will take the ravines inherited from this inauspicious event beyond our mortality. The avalanche of pain that swiftly covered our home will melt away and flow down the gutters of time. New memories will emerge like vegetation following thawing of deep frozen ice in the Arctic. However, some will have unwillingly donated limbs in the brink of death frosts. This ordeal made us pant for breath.

The atria and ventricles of my heart have lost their biological time clock as the sinews became flexed. The powerhouse, my brain, is discharging erroneous messages depriving systems and biological clock rhythms the maintenance of sanity. My feet are sore as those of one who has traversed the scorching desert sand on bare feet. The soles are cracked leaving behind a trail of marks on the ground where I have walked. My palate and throat are dry. I have transpired and donated much of my bodily fluid to the atmosphere. I desperately wish to tread upon an occasional oasis to cool myself. All these have contributed in modelling my history and arduous autobiography of misery.

Every day, every hour, every minute, and every second as the sun takes its inconspicuous journey across the sky, my life is sucked away with a new speck of faith incurred. Hence, our days become shorter as we grow in faith and leadership along the journey of life. To all those who are going through various difficulties in life, be steadfast and be of good hope, for the future will wipe away the dreadful past as it brings new events to the present!

I have watched and listened to priests recite these incantations: "A thousand years in the eyes of the Lord are like a mere yesterday. Men born of women live for a few days and they are no more!" Today I understand the depth of the words and the message they convey— that in heaven a thousand years are no more than a single day on earth. What an awful revelation, the speed at which time really moves! Lord, reveal to me the purpose for which I was created; help me live to my full potential while remaining a humble servant to humanity!

My boat was rocked, and I was in danger of sinking. For a moment I thought my Master was asleep and I was about to perish. But today I am amazed at what kind of man my Master is—the one who even the winds and the waves obey! The same adversities may have come into your life; you may be negotiating rough waves that siphon all hope from your sinews, but do not lose your faith and hope. Call out to the Master, and He will save you!

If rescue does not come forth at your expected time, remember how at Gethsemane our Lord began the last part of His painful journey. He prayed until His sweat became droplets of blood (A very rare medical condition known as *hematidrosis*). Through His trial and onerous torture all the way to the cross at Calvary, it seemed the heavens were silent! Before He gave a last breath, He called out, *"Eloi, Eloi, lama sabachthani?"* ("My God, why have You forsaken Me?"). You may be going through a situation in your life now, and it looks like you are abandoned and forgotten. He is very much alive and watching over you! You will soon arise from your grave of hunger, ill-treatment, poverty, and all kinds of suffering and pain!

According to some texts, there has not been born a prophet like Moses, whom the Lord knew face to face, none like him for all the signs and wonders which the Lord sent him to perform in Egypt and all the mighty power and the great and terrible deeds that he wrought in the sight of Israel.

The exodus of the Israelites from Egypt pioneered a very important feast in religion: the Passover event, which involved the killing of lambs and smearing of blood on door posts. This event set the Israelites free from the house of bondage. The incident is analogous with the death of Christ, who liberated nations from the bondage of sin through His blood. Instead of doors, only one post—the cross—was daubed with the blood of the Lamb for liberation of humankind as a whole. Today in the midst of Satanism and other evils, let us mark the doors of our hearts with His blood. The Son of Man began a new journey, one that leads to a different promised land—the land of eternal life, the land forfeited by our father Adam after he was stripped of the glory of the Lord and was found naked. Christ said that He is the way, the truth, and the life. He clearly stated that no one can get to the Father except through Him.

In about 1200 BC, a large army of armed men crossed the Jordan River into Canaan. They were followed by their women, children, and livestock. The shallow point where they crossed was located several miles north of the Dead Sea, about the same distance southeast of the ancient town of Jericho. On reaching the western bank, the convoy paused and gave thanks to Yahweh. At last they had entered the land He had promised them. They had finally made it back to Canaan, the land of their forefathers, following four hundred years of exile and hardship. Over forty years, Moses had forged them into a nation. However, Joshua was leading them into the Promised Land.

It is important to note that despite all the troubles we have been through, and despite their duration, we too will finally be back to Canaan where we belong. The Lord will hand over to us cities that we don't deserve, not because of our righteousness but because of His eternal love and mercy and our obedience. One day we will sing songs of victory like the Israelites did and say:

> Give thanks to the LORD, because he is good;
> his love is eternal.
> Give thanks to the greatest of all Gods;
> his love is eternal.
> Give thanks to the mightiest of all lords;
> his love is eternal.
> He alone performs great miracles;
> his love is eternal.
> By his wisdom he made the heavens;

his love is eternal;
He built the earth on the deep waters;
his love is eternal.
He made the sun and the moon;
his love is eternal;
the sun to rule over the day;
his love is eternal;
The moon and the stars to rule over the night;
His love is eternal.
He killed the first-born sons of the Egyptians;
his love is eternal.
He led the people of Israel out of Egypt;
his love is eternal;
with his strong hand, his powerful arm;
his love is eternal.
He divided the red sea;
his love is eteranal;
he let his people through it;
his love is eternal;
but he drowned the king of Egypt and his army;
his love is eternal.
He let his peole through the desert;
his love is eternal.
He killed powerful kings;
his love is eternal;
he killed famous kings;
his love is eternal;
Sihon, king of the Amorites;
his love is eternal;
and Og, king of Bashan;
his love is eternal.
He gave their lands to his people;
his love is eternal;
he gave them to Israel, his servant;

his love is eternal.
He did not forget us when we were defeated;
his love is eternal;
he freed us from our enemies;
his love is eternal.
He gives food to every living creature;
his love is eternal.
Give thanks to the God of heaven;
his love is eternal. (Psalm 136 TEV)

The journey of Israel ended with the conquest of Canaan, the Promised Land. However, their settling on this land required a certain code of conduct from them. There were still challenges that stretched out ahead of them. They had the ark of the covenant to constantly remind them where they came from and whose they were. They were given commandments and the law through Moses in the desert. Their surviving or perishing depended on their faithfulness and obedience to the law. It is important therefore to remember that the Lord has led you through difficult situations and settled you where you are! As you settle, remain faithful and keep His law. Then you will be prosperous in the land you have just taken possession of. You might have got a job, landed a promotion, just got married, been elected into power; know it is the Lord who has put you there! Please keep His law!

During his last days Joshua told the Israelites that he was old and well advanced in years. He retold the story of how the Lord had defeated nations for His people's sake. Joshua impressed on them that it was the Lord who had fought for Israel all the time. Joshua told his people to be very steadfast, to keep and do all that was written in the book of the Law of Moses, turning aside from it neither to the right hand nor to the left. It was important for them to remain watchful, not to be mixed with the nations left among them or make mention of the names of their gods, or swear by them, or serve them, or bow down to them, but to cleave unto the Lord their God as they had done thus far.

The Law

Chapter 3

The Israelites who entered Canaan were structured and devoted. On their way to the Promised Land, they might have been joined by new followers. These were social outcasts like themselves, who were attracted by Moses' proclamation of faith and hope. These newcomers provided an invaluable commitment to the Israelite cause. They provided an important encouragement to Joshua's juvenile army during its first battles in Canaan.

The outcasts were attracted to the Israelite religion by a number of things. In this era, the gods of every nation seemed to be concerned only about the rich and powerful. In Israel's God, they found a prominent defender of the weak. He had phenomenally delivered an oppressed people from slavery and aided their survival under harsh desert conditions. He seemed in their eyes able to control what events time brought to the present, according to His wishes.

In exchange for His favour, the God of Israel demanded (and still demands) complete loyalty not only to a set of rituals but to a basic system of laws. Originating from the Mosaic covenant between the Lord and Israel, these laws were specifically formulated to promote justice and personal freedom among the Israelites—for example, those dealing with land ownership and government. Such laws were unusual within the religious and social practice of the day.

In today's world, there is a myriad of laws. Some are international laws, while others are state laws promulgated by individual states.

Unfortunately, sometimes those who develop these laws are seeking to promote their own agendas. Other instruments are put in place but are badly implemented, and often the poor and feeble become victims of the rich and powerful. This preferential system has resulted in an aberration of law enforcement that has made the world a very dangerous place, especially to the weak. In fact, "the law of the jungle" defining survival of the fittest aptly characterizes many legal systems today. Doesn't today's world or system of governance find value in the Sinai covenant and its set of non-preferential laws handed over to Moses?

According to the Bible (Ex. 20: 1–2, NLT), the covenant begins as follows: "I am the Lord your God, who rescued you from the land of Egypt, the place of your slavery." In today's world we are in different forms of slavery. Our Egypt may not be a physical land like the one that enslaved the Israelites. On the other hand, our troubles, our poverty, our debts, our evil thoughts, and all sorts of sin constitute our house of bondage. The Son of Man died for us on the cross at Calvary so that we may be liberated from our burden.

"You must not have any other god but me" (vs. 3). Like the Canaanite deities that lured the Israelites from their worship of the Lord, in today's life, we are attracted by a different form of idols. We idolize people for varied reasons; we idolize money and other possessions. This has led to Satanism, where people perform acts of alarming abomination against members of the human race.

"You must not make for yourself an idol of any kind or an image of anything in the heavens or on the earth or in the sea. You must not bow down to them or worship them, for I, the Lord your God, am a jealous God who will not tolerate your affection for any other gods" (vss. 4–5). In Luke 4: 1–13, we read that the devil took Jesus up onto a mountain and revealed to Him all the kingdoms of the world and promised to give them to Him if He would worship him. Then Jesus replied that the scriptures say one must worship only the Lord and serve only Him. Exodus 20: 5–6 continues, "I lay the sins of the parents upon their children; the entire family is affected—even children in the third and fourth generations of those who reject me. But I lavish unfailing love for a thousand generations on those who love me and obey my commands." Hence, in John 9: 2 (NLT), the disciples ask, "Why was this man born blind? Was it because of his own sins or his parents' sins?" Jesus answered them that it was neither because of his sins or his parents' sins; but this had happened so that the power of the Lord could be seen in him. Therefore, in our troubles and sorrow, let us not be quick to judge that it might be because of our bad ancestry. It may simply be the Lord's plan to reveal His power through our predicaments.

"You must not misuse the name of the Lord your God. The Lord will not let you go unpunished if you misuse His name" (Ex. 20: 7). The devil took Jesus to the highest point of the temple in Jerusalem, and asked him to jump off if he truly was the Son of God, for God would order His angels to protect Him and hold Him up with their hands. However, Jesus answered that the scripture said you must not test the Lord your God. There are many Christian-based denominations preaching and proclaiming faith healing today. It is not that they are doing a bad thing, but the problem is that the sole purpose of some who claim to be faith healers is to venerate themselves and make money out of it. The reality is that such workers are just crooks who are misusing the name of the Lord.

When Paul, Barnabas, and Mark were in Cyprus during Paul's first missionary journey, they clashed with a Jewish magician named Bar-Jesus at the palace of the Roman proconsul, Sergius Paulus. Eager to keep his influence with the proconsul, Bar-Jesus tried to keep Paul and his company from proclaiming their faith. Paul glared at him and said, "You son of the devil … will you not stop making crooked the straight paths of the Lord? And now, behold, the hand of the Lord is upon you, and you will be blind." The terrified magician was led away sightless (Acts 13: 4–12, ESV).

In Acts 8: 5–20 is related how Philip went to Samaria and preached the good news about the Messiah. He cast out demons in the name of Jesus and many listened to him in great interest. The lame and paralyzed were healed. A famous sorcerer named Simon had lived there for many years, amazing the Samaritans and claiming to be a great person. Everyone from the community often referred to him as "the Great One—the Power of God" (vs. 10, NLT). They listened carefully to him since for a long time he had amazed them with his magic.

The people were now drawn by the good news told by Philip concerning the kingdom of the Father and His Son. Many men and women became converts and were baptized. Simon the sorcerer too became a convert and was baptized. He followed Philip wherever he went and was amazed by the miracles Philip performed in the name of Jesus.

When the apostles heard that the Samaritans had accepted the Lord Jesus, they sent Peter and John to Samaria. On arriving there, Peter and John laid hands on the new converts and prayed for them to receive the Holy Spirit. The Holy Ghost had not descended upon any of the new believers for they had only been baptized in the Lord Jesus' name. When Simon saw that the Spirit was given when the apostles laid their hands on people, he offered them money to buy the power of the Holy Spirit so that he too could lay hands on people and give them the Holy Spirit. Peter answered him, "May you and your money go to hell, for thinking that you can buy God's gift with money!" (Acts 8: 20 TEV). We must not misuse the name of the Lord our Ruler lest we suffer his punishment!

In Acts 19: 11–16 the Bible says that Paul was given power to perform unusual miracles. When handkerchiefs and aprons that had merely touched his skin were placed on sick people, they were healed of their diseases, and evil spirits were expelled. At the same time a group of Jews went from town to town casting out evil spirits. They tried to use the name of the Lord Jesus in their invocations. Seven sons of a prominent priest Sceva were doing this. On one of the occasions when they tried it, the evil spirit replied that it knew both Jesus and Paul, but it did not know them. Then the man with the evil spirit leaped on them, overpowered them, and attacked them with such vigour that they fled from the house naked and tattered. Therefore we must refrain from misusing the name of the Lord!

"Remember to observe the Sabbath day by keeping it holy" (Ex. 20: 8, NLT). To paraphrase verses 9–11, the Lord has given us six days each week for our ordinary work, but the seventh day is a Sabbath day of rest dedicated to the Lord our God. On that day no one in our household may do any work. This includes our sons and daughters, our male and female servants, our livestock, and any foreigners living in our midst. For it is said in six days the Lord made the heavens, the earth, the sea, and everything in them; but on the seventh day he rested. That is why the Lord blessed the Sabbath day and designated it as holy.

Since the Sabbath is holy, is it not the day when the Lord's miracles and favours should be expected? In Matthew 12: 1–8, it is said that Jesus was walking through some grain fields on the Sabbath. His disciples began to pick and eat some heads of grain as they were hungry. Some Pharisees complained that the disciples were harvesting grain on the Sabbath. Jesus reminded them that David and his companions ate the sacred loaves of bread reserved to be eaten only by priests. He went on to cite a section in the Law of Moses that allows the priests on duty in the temple to work on a Sabbath. He told them that amongst them there was one who was even greater than the temple. The Son of Man is Lord over everything, even over the Sabbath.

Jesus went on to pose questions to the Pharisees. He asked them whether they would not work to pull out their sheep if it had fallen into a well on the Sabbath, and affirmed to them that they would. He pointed out that people are much more valuable than sheep and that the law does permit people to do good things on a Sabbath.

The Pharisees were a group of people who wanted to use the law for their own convenience. They did not fear the Lord who gave the law but pretended to obey the law. All laws should be instruments to guide people, not to oppress them. As such, they should apply uniformly to the poor or rich, peasants and elite. It is an unfortunate reality that even today, to many of us, our property is considered to be more important than our fellow human beings.

The world has come to a state where we think that our money can buy us freedom. We should be aware that there is no freedom when one is not spiritually free. Jesus' love is amazing. The Lord loved the world through Him. He is the Redeemer, who came so that all may be saved.

Do we place more importance on our laws than we do to those of the Lord? I remember in South Africa, during the times of apartheid, a common sight was a white person driving a van with black "boys" sitting in the load bin while a dog peeped through the window in the same compartment with "boss." I could not help but wonder how the people who had brought the Bible to Africa could act in such a manner. How did those who were involved in these deeds read and interpret its message? I naively thought that every white person must have been a person of biblically based faith.

A Pharisee today is a person who knows and even teaches the law but does not practice it. At many churches that preach the gospel, as ministers we fail dismally to practice what we preach! For whom is our message meant then? Everybody who holds the Bible in their left hand and performs evil deeds with their right hand is acting against the law of the Lord! It is time for us to resolve to practise what we preach.

In some of His teachings (see Matthew 23) Jesus taught that the scribes and the Pharisees sit on Moses' seat. He urged the people to practice and do what the scribes and Pharisees told them but not follow their deeds, for they preached but did not practice. They bound heavy burdens, hard to bear, and lay them on men's shoulders; but they themselves would not move them with their finger. They did all their deeds to be seen by men; for they made their phylacteries broad and their fringes long, and they loved the place of honour at feasts and the best seats in the synagogues, salutations in the marketplaces, and being called rabbi by men. He told people that they were not to be called rabbi; for they had one teacher and they were all brethren. He called the scribes and Pharisees hypocrites because they shut the kingdom of heaven against men; for they neither entered themselves, nor allowed those who would enter to go in. He called them blind guides who understood that if anyone swore by the temple it was all right; but if anyone swore by the gold of the temple, they were bound by their oath. He referred to them as blind fools for they could not grasp that the temple was greater than gold, because the temple made the gold sacred. Which one is greater, the flesh or the spirit that lives on following mortal death?

Our world is no different. We perform elaborate gestures to be recognized by the multitudes, and yet we do nothing towards pleasing our Creator. We enjoy being praised and followed by a harem of women while brandishing our material wealth. If only as men we would please the Lord as we are prepared to please the world, then we would make it a better place.

In Mathew 11: 28–30, Jesus encourages anyone who is tired from carrying heavy burdens to come to Him. He promises that He will give us rest. He is asking us to take His yoke and put it on ourselves. He wants us to learn from Him because He is gentle and humble in spirit; and therefore in Him we will find rest. For the yoke He will give to us is easy, and the load He will put on us is light. Many of the leaders of this world tell their followers to do as they say but not as they do. Indeed the laws of this world put heavy loads on men. Surprisingly, even those who are advocates of these laws might not carry the burden if the tables were to turn. In many states, cruel laws have been enacted that have led to the demise of multitudes. Apart from laws, the world has made us carry heavy burdens. Some are burdens of starvation and poverty; others are burdens of debt, desire, jealousy, anger from the past, fear, sickness, fighting, pride, hatred … the list is long. Let us come to Him, for He is gentle in spirit, and His yoke is light. He is calling now, and to follow Him there is no heavy payment required. He just needs our inner self!

"Honour your father and mother. Then you will live a long, full life in the land the Lord your God is giving you" (Ex. 20: 12, NLT). In the Bible, a man named Manoah from the tribe of Dan did not have children with his wife. One day the angel of the Lord appeared to his wife and told her that she would soon fall pregnant with a baby son. She was not to drink wine or eat any forbidden food. The angel went on to tell her that the baby would be named Samson. Samson's mother was given instructions that her son's hair was not be cut from birth, as he would be a Nazirite, and he would also not drink any alcohol. Samson would rescue Israel from the Philistine oppression which had taken forty years.

Samson's encounter with the Philistines began when he fell in love with a woman from Timnah (Judges 14: 1–5). Timnah was a Philistine-controlled village which lay across from Zorah which was Samson's home. On one occasion when Samson returned from

Timnah, he presented his parents with a shocking and insistent request. He explained that he would like to get married to a Philistine woman from Timnah. His parents refused and wanted to know why he couldn't get a wife from his own people, as was customary. Samson ignored his parents and went on with his plans.

One can imagine Samson giving his parents the following response, as it is common amongst today's youth: "It is my life! You are old-fashioned! I am in love with this woman! Who are you to stop me from getting married to her? Stop running my life! It is my right! No girl has ever touched me like her!" Such arguments are common even from our kids today. They do not know that their parents are experienced in life, and they have seen it all. So Samson went to Timnah to arrange and hold his wedding feast there, in defiance of his parents who would not let him hold the celebration in their home. Eventually Samson got married to this Philistine, although unfortunate circumstances let to her death.

Samson's obsession with Philistine women made him later fall in love with the prostitute Delilah from the Sorek valley. The Philistine rulers went to Delilah and asked her to beg Samson to reveal the secret of his power. They promised to give Delilah 1,100 pieces of silver each. So Delilah persuaded her lover to tell her what it would take to tie him up securely. Following a number of deceits, Samson finally gave away the secret that from birth he had never cut his hair.

Delilah then soothed Samson to sleep on her lap and called a man to cut the seven locks on Samson's hair. Then she began to torment him, for his strength had left him. Then the Philistines gouged out his eyes and brought him down to Gaza. He was bound with bronze chains and made to grind grain in prison (Judges 16: 18–21).

Oh dear, if only he had honoured his parents, who were given the full story on what kind of person he would become and what he was supposed to do. They had told him the story of how Israel were sojourners in the land of Egypt and how the Lord had rescued them through the hand of Moses. They had related the story of how Samson's ancestors had died in the desert due to their disobedience to the Lord. They explained to him the Lord's covenant with Israel and its conditions. Nonetheless, the beauty he saw in Philistine women made him blind and deaf. Their eyes, hairstyles, curves, voices, shape, bombshell walks, and warmth knocked sense out of him. "Honour your father and mother ..."

My friend, my sister, my brother, and my child, I am making a solemn appeal to you: Where are you now? Have you run away from your parents to take refuge on Delilah's lap? You are resting at a wrong place! Get away before you give away the sacred secret! Go away while you still have your eyes! Those drugs and parties will gouge out your eyes! Go back to school and learn; you have a bright future ahead of you.

The apostle Paul, in his letter to the Ephesians (6: 1–3), encourages children to obey their parents because they belong to the Lord, and that this is the right thing to do. Honour your father and mother. This is the first commandment with a promise: If you honour your father and mother, things will go well for you, and you will have a long life on earth. Paul goes on to say that fathers should not provoke their children to anger by the way they treat them. Fathers should rather bring their children up with the discipline and instruction that comes from the Lord. Note that the Lord brings children onto the earth and He knows what they will grow up to become, provided they are brought up with his discipline and instructions.

"You must not murder" (Ex. 20: 13, NLT). We saw what happened to Cain and how he was punished for murdering his brother Abel. It was said that the land he tilled would no more produce crops. In the world in which we live today, murder has become normal. Women and children are raped and killed. The whole world is sick! People kill each other as if it were fun. The world is hit by economic depression, hunger, and poverty, and it has lost most of its production; yet it is hard for anyone to turn to the Lord. For many it is still considered a weakness to kneel and pray to the Lord.

The pressures of life have forced us into selfish behaviour. We are asking the Lord the same selfish question: are we our brothers' guardians? Yes, we are supposed to be mutual guardians by looking after one another. What is there to gain by killing our brothers? The Lord knows when we are wronged, and He recompenses us. By trying to get our own justice, we are drawn deep into sin; sometimes we come out worse than those who did us wrong.

In Luke 17: 1–2, Jesus told his disciples that there would always be temptations to sin, but the great sorrow awaits the person who does the tempting. In Matthew 5: 21–22 He says that our ancestors were told not to murder and that if they committed murder they were subject to judgement. However, He said that if we are even angry with someone, we are subject to judgement. Therefore we must learn to subdue anger and to be its masters. When we are angry with someone, we surely do not think well of them, and we may even harm them.

"You must not commit adultery" (Ex. 20: 14, NLT). In Matthew 19: 1–9, some Pharisees tried to trap Jesus by asking him whether a man should be allowed to divorce his wife for any reason at all. Jesus replied to them by asking whether they had read the scriptures which say, from the beginning God created a woman and a man. He made them one. That is why a man leaves his father and mother and is joined to his wife, and the two are united as one. Since they are no longer two but one, no one may split what the Lord has put together! The Law of Moses permitted divorce as a compromise due to Israel's hard hearts. But, it is not what the Lord intends. Then Jesus told them that whoever divorces his wife and marries someone else commits adultery—unless his wife has been unfaithful.

According to Jesus' teaching, a man who looks at a woman with lust has already committed adultery with her in his heart. It follows that our thinking is crucially important. The more we dwell on certain thoughts, the more they become imprinted in our brains. Once impressed onto our brains, these thoughts become part of us wherever we go, so that we end up acting on them automatically. Hence the saying, "As a man thinks, so he is." The more we think deeply about something in desire, we become part of it in spirit and invite it to come to pass, since our thoughts are not limited by time or distance.

In our day what does this mean? Have we read and understood the scripture about the creation of man and woman? Whose creatures are we, and whose laws do we obey? Are the laws that control the universe against the laws of the Creator? But our heavenly Father created the universe and all the laws that govern it. There are times when as humans we go against the laws of the universe, but the question is, can we prevail? Human laws grant freedom for people to go against the laws of nature, calling such freedoms *rights*. If human rights are contrary to the laws of creation, are they correct?

As we know, various reasons may lead to divorce and adultery. The primary reasons that draw people to one another so that they end up getting married may lead to their divorce and adultery. Some of us get into marriage because we have met someone rich, famous, or occupying a high position in society, while others are ensnared by physical appearance. These things are not bad if they are not the sole impulse uniting those who enter into marriage. On the other hand, if the union of those getting married is driven by these things, they are bound to part along the way as, in life, time presents us with different events. One individual may be rich at a particular time, and circumstances may change in the same life. Likewise, one's physical appearance may be altered by age or accidents. Does that mean we will have to run away from our partners?

If we use our partners as shelter or a cave during adverse weather, we need to know that the storm will be over and the chilly nights will end; then we will leave them, for they will have outlasted their usefulness. The question is; do we remain faithful and united to our partners even under the worst of conditions? I know people who have got married to others because of rich family backgrounds, and when life presents challenges they part ways. For the gold mine they saw in their partners has become depleted of resources. There are couples whose happiness and unity are chiefly dependent on the financial status of the other partner. However, on the day of their union in marriage couples swear, "For richer, for poorer ... till death do us part." Let us remember that when we take these oaths, we take them in the presence of the Lord, with humans present only as witnesses.

A classic example is the story of Job, the servant of the Lord. Job meticulously served the Lord and offered sacrifices to Him. The Lord allowed Satan to test him first by taking all his material riches and children. Then Satan made sores break all over Job's body. Job's wife turned against him at this difficult time and asked him to curse the Lord and die. Oh Father, during the time when everything went well, Job was referred to as "daddy" and "sweetheart," "love of my life," a "match made in heaven." In times of trouble he was called a "good for nothing dog," and his wife may have asked, "Why did I ever get married to you? I need to find a better man who can even satisfy my needs, for you have been reduced to this unattractive scrap infested with sores. A man I once loved has been reduced to a shadow of himself."

All these things are familiar and relevant in our lives today! When they happen, we must be strong in faith and look up to our Father who is ever watching over us! Sometimes we do not have to make a move but simply turn everything over to Him and wait. Remember, He is in control over what time brings to our present.

I have already referred to losing my job at the end of the year 2009. Immediately following that in 2010, I lost huge sums of money through fraud. As I was trying to cope with joblessness and debts, I lost a driver and friend, and my two daughters in a tragic head-on collision accident on 4 June 2011. It is during such times that one's heat oppressed brains may lead them into thinking that the Lord has ceased existing! We must be drawn to Him because we understand His love and because we truly love Him. Our faith must not be premised on a chase for material blessings and desires. When the Son of Man gave His life for humanity on the cross at Calvary, it was not because He was compelled to do so but because of His unconditional love.

"You must not steal" (Ex. 20: 15, NLT). In Leviticus 6: 1–7, the Lord explained to Moses that if one amongst the people were to sin against their associate and become unfaithful to the Lord; or if anyone cheated in a deal involving a security deposit, or stole or committed fraud, or found lost property and lied about it, or lied while swearing to tell the truth, or committed any other such sin, they were guilty. They were to give back whatever they stole or the money they had acquired by extortion, the security deposit, the lost property they had found, or anything obtained by swearing falsely. They had to make restitution by paying the full price plus an additional 20 percent to the person they had harmed. On the same day, they had to present a guilt offering.

It is amazing how some of our nations use the Bible when swearing leaders into positions, and we often hear those who are sworn in say, "So help me God." It is following such ceremonies that we usually do the opposite of what we promised. We get into positions and become unfaithful not only to those we lead but to ourselves and the Lord. We start moving around with entourages of guards and convoys of vehicles while embezzling public funds and treating badly the same people we have to serve. Are we simply taking these oaths in order to secure positions, or do we honestly not understand what we are doing? Leadership is about service and not about being served.

Some of us desperately look for jobs. However, after we have secured a job, we start stealing from our masters. Please let us be informed that we are actually stealing from the Lord, who is our sole provider. The Bible says in Ephesians 6: 5–9, that slaves should obey their earthly masters with profound reverence and trepidation. Slaves must serve their masters sincerely as they would serve the Lord. They must try to please their masters all the time, not just when they are under supervision.

As slaves of the Lord, we must do what He desires with all our heart. We must work eagerly with interest, as though we were working for the Lord rather than for people. We must remember that the Lord will recompense each one of us according to the good we do, whether we are slaves or free. Masters should also treat their slaves in the same way; they should not intimidate them. Remember, we all have the same Master in heaven to whom exaltation and veneration are truly due, and He has no preferential treatment.

It is common to see street vendors in our towns selling stolen goods. If you talk to some of them, they say, "I have stolen it from my boss. He [or she] has a lot of money!" In doing so, do we realize we are destroying our own jobs? If your boss eventually goes bankrupt, do you understand that not only you and your family will suffer, but your boss and many other families who depended on the thriving of that business? One day, in one of the towns, a man selling stolen spectacles approached me to try and sell to me. He offered a pair to me for a hundred and fifty rand (R150.00). When I looked at the original price per pair the tag showed eight hundred and fifty rand (R850.00). When I asked the man where he had got the spectacles from, he said that he had stolen them from his workplace. He was working for a white business, and according to him it was a good thing to steal from a white business, and he thought that I would support him.

I talked to him and showed him that he was destroying not only his job but jobs for others. I then asked him whether he would be happy to have people do the same to his business the day he owns one. He replied that he would not be happy. Then I asked him why he was doing it to others! He was frightened and thought that I would call the police! I told him to stop what he was doing. He left me scared and showing great remorse, and I did not buy from him. I did not want to be an accomplice in the eyes of our Creator for inflicting pain by providing a market for stolen goods. Please note that the commandment does not beg us to stop stealing, but it strongly says, "You must not steal!"

"You must not testify falsely against your neighbour" (Ex. 20: 16, NLT). Although this commandment specifies "neighbour," what it means is anyone at all. It is common that when we need favour with others, we start giving false testimony about our fellow humans. In Genesis 39, Potiphar's wife gave false testimony about Joseph, and he ended up in prison for a crime he did not commit. The same thing happened with Jesus of Nazareth, who was falsely accused by the Jews and put to death.

It is good to look for promotion at work as long as it comes as a result of our genuine effort. It is also common that workers bad-mouth others so that they end up laid off from their jobs. If you love your children, look at them and think about what would become of them if you were to lose everything. Then why would you want others to lose everything due to your false testimony? Their children are as important as yours.

Many of us have been acquitted by earthly courts through good defences by our lawyers, and yet we know that we have committed the act. The world may set us free but if we remain guilty under the universal law that will be used for our judgement in the world to come, does it help us in any way to temporarily and falsely win hearts of men? Let us always fear the One who has power to judge and condemn both flesh and spirit.

The commandments end by saying, "**You must not covet your neighbour's house. You must not covet your neighbour's wife, male or female servant, ox or donkey, or anything else that belongs to your neighbour**" (Ex. 20: 17, NLT). In short, this commandment asks us to wish others well on what they have. We must not wish it were ours, for that is when we start being consumed by jealousy and even devise means to get what does not belong to us. I know people who say, "I will make that man [or woman] mine against all odds!"

There are those who use their power to commit evil deeds. In 1 Kings 11, King David of Israel coveted the wife of Uriah the Hittite, Bathsheba. David plotted and carried out Uriah's murder with the sword of the Ammonites. When we are in power, it does not mean that we may keep everything that we want for ourselves. We must learn to wish others well on what they have. As a consequence of doing so, the good we wish on them comes to us.

Jesus came to fulfil the law and to show how people should obey the law of the Father by setting practical examples. He said that we must not misunderstand why He had come. For instance, He did not come to put an end to the Law of Moses and the writings of the prophets. He confirmed that he came to give full meaning to the

Law and the prophetic writings. "I tell you the truth, until heaven and earth disappear, not even the smallest detail of God's law will disappear until its purpose is achieved" (Matthew 5: 18, NLT)." He said that if we close the eyes to the least commandment and instruct others to follow us, we will be regarded the least in the kingdom of heaven. Amazingly, it is a common human nature that when people go astray, they want others to follow in their footsteps and support them. It is one thing to picket and demonstrate for grievances, but to mobilize and engage in wicked acts and destroy lives and property is unlawful in the eyes of the Lord.

Jesus' famous teaching, the Sermon on the Mount, particularly the opening portion that we know as the Beatitudes (Matthew 5: 3–12, TEV), encapsulates the whole law as follows.

"Happy are those who know they are spiritually poor; the Kingdom of heaven belongs to them!" We often mistakenly think that simply being subjected to poverty entitles us to the kingdom of heaven. Spiritual poverty refers to internal poverty; those with this quality do not exalt themselves but truly feel that they are nothing and can do nothing without Jehovah. It is when we feel that we are least that our Father in heaven reaches out, lifts, and spiritually enriches us. In our pride, where we feel that we possess certain spiritual gifts, the Lord watches and leaves us alone to do that which we think we know. Although Jesus was begotten and always had the glory of the Father, He assumed the position of a servant amongst men, whereas humans naturally like to talk and brag about their knowledge, gifts, talents, positions, and wealth.

"Happy are those who mourn; God will comfort them!" We are aggrieved by different situations in life. And yet if we do what the Lord requires, our groans will be turned to happiness. God sees every unfavourable situation, every hurt, mistreatment, and injustice we ever come across. We may be mourning due to various circumstances; a loss of a loved one or any other calamity that time may have brought our way. Wherever we may be, it is important to remember that we have a Father who never fails—not ever!

"Happy are those who are humble; they will receive what God has promised!" Humility is like spiritual poverty. The truly humble are those who do not fight back or take revenge when they are wronged. They just trust in the Lord to deliver His promise at the correct time. These are the people who do not show off. Like the spiritually poor, they are not full of pride. Even when they have done something good, such people do not accept praise from the world. They maintain their silence and would prefer that the good they have done should be discovered by chance. These are the people who turn the other cheek. It is not easy to reach this level in faith.

"Happy are those whose greatest desire is to do what God requires; God will satisfy them fully!" Our greatest desire on earth should be to do what our Creator requires. He wants us to be faithful. He does not want us to kill each other. He is displeased by arrogance, jealousy, adultery, idolatry, theft, cruelty, greed, and lack of respect for others. In Luke 3: 10–14, different categories of people want to know what they must do to be safe. John the Baptist tells those who have plenty to give to the needy, tax collectors to collect what is stipulated by the law, and soldiers to be content with what they are paid. All these three things one may not achieve without love and mercy. In many governments around the world, officials take bribes while their masters steal public funds in the rat race to riches. Many of them never really see prosperity with this stolen money.

"Happy are those who are merciful to others; God will be merciful to them!" It is startling how even those who have killed others will wail and ask for mercy when faced with danger. When Cain was beating his brother Abel to death, he did not listen when his brother asked for mercy. Amazingly, after God announced the judgement to Cain, he cried that he would be killed by beasts. What selfishness! There are men who have ruled over others in this world and committed atrocities against others without mercy. When they are brought to justice, they cry for mercy! How hard is it for us to realize when others truly require our compassion! The powerful in this world have tortured men and women and gloried over their incarceration, but when they have to undergo similar conditions, they wail bitterly as it were doomsday.

"Happy are the pure in heart; they will see God!" The pure in heart do not have evil thoughts, for the seed of sin starts with thought. A pure heart does not entertain greed, evil desires, or any form of malice. Men and women with pure hearts work for the good of others in their communities. They do not use others for their own benefit and then dump them. These are men and women who strive and work for peace. That is why the apostle Paul, in Philippians 2: 14–15, urged people to do everything without complaints or arguments so that they could be innocent and pure as the Lord's children. **"Happy are those who work for peace; God will call them his children!"**

"Happy are those who are persecuted because they do what God requires; the Kingdom of heaven belongs to them!" The world hates the truth. The world hates light. The world is full of injustice. At workplaces, in communities, in churches, and within families there is persecution. Those who are truly children of the Lord are a thorn to those who serve their father, Satan. Therefore, **"Happy are you when people insult you and persecute you and tell all kinds of evil lies against you because you are my followers. Be happy and glad, for a great reward is kept for you in heaven. This is how the prophets who lived before you were persecuted."**

Remember how the prophet Elijah was persecuted by King Ahab and his wife, Queen Jezebel (1 Kings 18: 40; 19: 2–3). After Elijah had killed the prophets of Baal at the River Kishon, Jezebel wanted to kill Elijah. The prophet fled to Beersheba where he wandered into the wilderness, sat under the shade of a tree, and wished he could die. He prayed to the Lord that he had had enough, so he could as well be dead.

Today you may feel the same way. The world has not done right by you. You are spiritually in the wilderness, where you think you could be better off dead! Do you hear the angel next to you? Can you feel his touch? If you listen carefully, he is saying that you must wake up and eat lest the journey becomes too much for you! If you carefully look around, amidst the persecutions; there is a loaf of bread next to you! Spiritual food from our Father will give you enough strength to walk the remaining days of your life!

Wherever troubles and persecutions have landed you, the Lord is asking: "What do you want here?" Listen closely, and you will hear the same soft voice that was in the beginning—yes, the same voice that gave all creation its shape, the voice that leads every step in our journey of life. You might be fighting against the spirit of Satanism that is trying to kill you or against depression or an ailment that threatens to take your life. Please wake up and eat, for you still have a long way to go! In Elijah's days, Israel had turned to worship the idol of Baal and other foreign deities. The people of the world today have turned against the Lord and broken the Golgotha covenant, the covenant through which men and women were bought with the blood of the Holy Lamb.

After Darius the Mede conquered Babylon, following the death of Belshazzar, because of Daniel's reliability, the king considered putting him in charge over the whole empire. Some of his officials plotted against Daniel, but they could not find any charge against him that would stick. So they asked the king to pass a decree declaring that for thirty days no one was to request anything from any god or human being except from the king, and they made the king sign the order. The order was considered a strict law of the Medes and Persians. When Daniel's enemies saw him praying to the Lord, they went and accused him before the king, who was upset and tried in vain to rescue Daniel. Daniel was arrested and put in the pit of lions, where not a single lion harmed him (Daniel 6: 1–28).

If we remain faithful in our organizations despite persecutions, we will emerge winners. When we remain steadfast in the Lord's course, He will not let us be ruined by lions that surround us in our families and at the workplace. We must not lose our faith and lose direction in the middle of trouble. It is through these persecutions that others will come to know the strength of the God we pray to; yes, the whole world will know that He alone is the living God, who will rule forever! His kingdom and power will never come to an end! He was in the beginning and the journey through the desert, He is here now, and He will be in the end, and all was created through Him!

This message is meant to bring peace and harmony across the whole world without prejudice. I do not see how any people of conscience may hate this sermon, whether they are followers of the Christian faith or not. Although the Law became prominent during Moses' time, there was law in the beginning given to Adam and Eve. Their transgressing of that law resulted in their expulsion from the garden of Eden. They were stripped of glory and made subordinate to other heavenly creatures. But because the Lord loved Adam and his posterity so much, He promised to erase his iniquity through the death of His Son and take him back to paradise.

In Deuteronomy 10: 12–21, Moses told the Israelites to listen to what the Lord their God demanded of them. He told the people to worship the Lord and obey all that He commanded, to love Him and serve Him with all their heart, and obey all His laws. Moses explained that to the Lord belong even the highest heavens; the earth and everything on it belongs to Him. The Lord's love for Israel's ancestors was so strong that he chose Israel instead of any other people. The Lord is supreme over all gods and powers. He is great and mighty and must be feared. He does not show partiality, and He does not accept bribes. He makes sure that orphans and widows are fairly treated. He loves foreigners living among our people and gives them food and clothes. Remember, to Him there is no foreigner, for He created the world and everything on it!

While the earth and all that is on it comes from the Lord, humans may decide to exploit anything on it unfairly without fear. If we serve the Lord faithfully, he will not let us go without food, or let us suffer without reason. The fact that we still live today proves His love and purpose. He is supreme over our earthly masters, and He does not administer partial justice. It may seem sometimes that we await the Lord's justice for a long time, but let us remember His plans are not ours, and to Him a thousand years is like a day. We are usually driven by our earthly desires where we end up looking for quick fixes. In the end there is no sustainability in these quick fixes, but the devil ends up pulling us into his dungeon of sin. I would like to appeal to the murderous who kill and mutilate innocent people and sell their parts for money, and to those who think they will be powerful through usage of concoctions made from human body parts. Since the beginning of life, the Lord has been saying, "Abide by My laws and commandments, and I will abundantly reward you!"

Of all laws and commandments, the greatest is that of love for the Lord and one another. Those who love one another will live in peace and harmony. That is why Jesus in John 15: 12–17 says His commandment is for us to love one another, just as He loved us. He explains that there is no greater love than that of a person who gives up his life for his friends. He therefore commands us to love one another.

There is a saying that "no man is an island." Whether we like it or not, we have to relate with other people in life to get what we want. In order to receive God's glory, we have to perform acts of love towards others. It might be through giving to the needy, listening to those who need to be heard, or taking part in solving various challenges that threaten human well-being. Without love for one another, it becomes very difficult to deal with other people unless the worst of scenarios forces us to come together. We must always try and do to others what we would like to be done on us.

Let us discover the book of the Law of the Lord and keep His laws and commandments. This will put an end to the wars in the Arab world, Africa, and everywhere else. In the eighteenth year of the rule of King Josiah of Judah, the book of the Law was discovered. When the book was read to King Josiah, he gave orders to his officials that they had to go and consult the Lord for him and for all the people of Judah about the teachings of the book. He explained that the Lord was angry with the people because their ancestors had not done what the book of the Law said ought to be done (2 Kings 22: 3–20).

As for today's generation, which book of the covenant are we using? Are we doing what this book says we must do? Let us do away with the idols of Baal and Asherah that dwell within our hearts. Let us burn down all these evil objects—lust, jealousy, evil desires, adultery, hijackings, drug abuse, and all sorts of cruelty against one another.

Through Moses the Lord had warned Israel that once they had settled in the Promised Land, they would request to have a king like the nations around them. Among the instructions were that the king was not to have many wives, for this would turn him away from the Lord; and he was not to enrich himself with silver and gold. Further, the king was to have a copy of the book of the Lord's laws. He was to keep this book next to him and read from it all his life so that he would learn to honour the Lord and faithfully obey everything commanded in the book. This would keep the king from thinking that he was better than his countrymen and from dishonouring the Lord's commands in any way.

It is important to note that the Lord is king over everything, but those on earth have chosen to set up their idolatry figures and to fear and serve them even more than we do to Him. Some of these figures are burdened with all sorts of crime. Idolized also are material goods; loving them lures us into a tangled web of iniquity. Many of us today are married to jealousy, crime, infidelity, and malice. All these things turn us from the Lord. We each have to ask ourselves these questions: Where is the book of the Lord's laws and commandments? Are we keeping this book next to us, reading from it, and practicing what it commands us to do? Why is it that we still think we are better than our fellow humans? Would we be involved in so many events of manslaughter taking place around the world, some of which arise as a result of some leaders who want to indefinitely anchor themselves to positions of power?

Hearken, oh sons of Adam, sons of Seth, sons of Kenan, sons of Enos, sons of Mahalalel, sons of Jared, sons of Enoch, sons of Methuselah, sons of Lamech, sons of Noah, sons of Shem, Ham, and Japheth: you all have the same blood, red in colour. You have been distributed throughout the whole world and have developed various phenotypes over the years to suit your environments, but that must not make you rivals unto death. You have become various nations and tribes. This should not be the reason for so much hatred and conflicts.

Put bluntly, is it the materials of the world that make us so arrogant and blind to the reality? In our death we retain no piece of these materials. Whether black or white, long- or short-haired, male or female, rich or poor, educated or illiterate, eating from the most expensive hotels or from dustbins, kings or peasants—we all breathe the same air and possess the same blood, and our bodies are mortal. The uprisings that sometimes result in genocides and brutal manslaughter achieve nothing in the end.

The weapons that we constantly improve for killing our fellow humans ... do they really help us achieve law and order? Nations approve heavy budgets towards development and improvement of deadly weapons while people die from hunger and pandemics. Yes, we have ended human lives! How is that an achievement when the next second we may just fall and die? Heavy budgets have been approved for building the most inhuman of prisons, and laws have been developed—one instrument after another—but are we really succeeding, or have we become instruments of the evil spirit? Perhaps if our success indicator was to fill as many prisons as possible in a certain time! Some of us go around guarded by men armed with dangerous weapons; does this guarantee us eternal life?

The foregoing brings us to the subjects of love and leadership. Do unto others what you would like them to do unto you: for this is the meaning of the law of the Lord handed down through Moses and of the teachings of the prophets!

> There is no condemnation now for those who live in union with Christ Jesus. For the law of the Spirit, which brings us life in union with Christ Jesus, has set me free from the law of sin and death. What the law could not do, because human nature was weak, God did. He condemned sin in human nature by sending his own Son, who came with a nature like sinful human nature, to do away with sin. God did this so that the righteous demands of the law might be fully satisfied in us who live according to the Spirit, and not according to human nature. Those who live as their human nature tells them to, have

their minds controlled by what human nature wants. Those who live as the Spirit tells them to, have their minds controlled by what the Spirit wants. To be controlled by human nature results in death; to be controlled by the Spirit results in life and peace. And so people become enemies of God when they are controlled by their human nature; for they do not obey God's law, and in fact they cannot obey it. Those who obey their human nature cannot please God. (Romans 8: 1–8, TEV)

Those who truly live according to the Holy Spirit may not be condemned. The reality is that the Spirit of the Father gives a person peace, mercy, forgiveness, love, integrity, and a fear of doing whatever displeases the Lord. Then if one lives according to the Holy Spirit, the sins of lust, theft, murder, falsehood, jealousy, and selfishness no longer have control over us. Therefore, if we are immune to these iniquities, the law cannot find fault with us. We can only be jailed through persecution by those who serve their father Satan! Since the Holy Spirit in us makes us die to the demands of the flesh, the law that controls the flesh no longer has control over us for our acts are those of the Father and the Son. Therefore if the Father and the Son be for us, all things in us work for good, and who dares be against us?

A painful reality the world faces today is that the rulers, the judges, the police, prison warders, counsellors, and most of us are not immune to criminal acts. The truth is that the man-made laws that rule the world today are manipulated by men for the desires of their flesh, which lead to death! If we were to live according to the Spirit, we would not need the law, since our flesh would totally submit to what our Father wants. Without the Holy Spirit, there is no hope for those who uphold the law. They are like the Pharisees of Jesus' time. Elders, lawyers, judges, police, and the rest are found raping, involved in drug deals, and ensnared in other corrupt acts when they are supposed to advocate for their eradication. Unless we suffer physically with Jesus, we remain involved with sin. The Law was given through Moses, but it was fulfilled through Jesus, the Lamb of God, who takes away the sin of the world.

Leadership

Chapter 4

Leadership is the ability of influencing others to follow you. Leadership has two sides to it. It may be bad or good depending on the views of those favouring and opposing it. Gangsters and drug lords look up to their leaders and aspire to become like them one day; those in various organizations breed followers who see them as models. On another level, there are men and women who aspire to be a Mother Teresa, a Princess Diana, a Winston Churchill, a Franklin D. Roosevelt, a Mao Zedong, a Mahatma Gandhi, or a Nelson Mandela. These are just a few examples of great men and women whose leadership model we may want to follow.

To be a leader, one should be influential and maintain integrity and discipline in one's course. As we have seen in the journey (chapter 2), leadership is also a journey, with challenges that require maintenance of integrity, discipline, and determination to continue leading towards a specific goal. Hence, a clear vision is important for a leader, for those who walk haphazardly in darkness may not reach a desired destination, and they impart their wobbly movement to their followers. Therefore a blind person may not lead another. It is also important to identify and groom potential leaders to continue the course, as in a relay race. Without a follower to take over, there is no success.

From ancient history we have heard of and we continue to experience various forms of leadership and leaders. How a leader influences his or her followers is the most important process that makes them go into historical record. In Lesotho, I have seen shepherds lead their flocks and herds to and from pastures. I did not realize the importance of this phenomenon until I started reading some leadership books. As the shepherds take their herds for grazing and back, they walk in front of the animals, while the animals follow them all the way and compete to be next to the herder. The herders do not drive the animals from behind!

Leadership is influenced by a number of factors, one of which is character integrity. Integrity in leadership is like the intact hull of a ship. Without holes, a ship remains afloat, and many journeys are accomplished. With holes, however, a ship may sail for a short distance but then start sinking with whatever is on board—whether people or merchandise or both—leaving their fate to depend on any rescue mission that may be launched. The time it takes to sink depends on the number and size of the holes and the weight of the ship. The more holes and the bigger the holes, the faster the ship sinks.

Likewise, if leaders act in ways that tarnish their image before their followers, they drill holes in their integrity, the only thing they can rely on to keep them afloat. When the actions of leaders rob their followers of confidence them, their =ability to lead dies out. Then it becomes very difficult to keep the ship afloat, and sailing soon becomes impossible.

Leadership may also compare to walking amongst thorny bushes with new clothes. If leaders walk carelessly so that their clothes are caught by the bushes, they will have donated pieces of cloth, and their bodies will be wounded and scarred. I have seen blankets of herders who stay at the cattle posts in my country, the seams of their blankets are scratched to frills by the bushes among which they daily walk. The problem can be solved by empowering these herders with the right protective clothing. In the same manner, leaders need to continuously be empowered with the right tools.

In leadership, there are various reasons why people follow a leader, and there are also many reasons why others may want to lead. I would like to mention the following three reasons why people follow and three reasons why people want to lead:

REASONS WHY PEOPLE MAY FOLLOW OTHERS

People follow because they see someone as able
to meet their needs and wants

In this category, the followers are either compelled by their needs to follow someone who may satisfy them, or they are misled by perceptions that they may hide behind the leader to fulfil their motives. People who belong to this category are like those who get into a relationship because they think their partner fulfils certain needs such as being a financial security or satisfying their desires. Such relationships never last because they depend on the status of the other party. Here one of two scenarios may take place: either the leader is genuinely devoted to the follower and is fully committed to the relationship, or the leader takes advantage of the weaknesses of the follower, making the follower an eternal slave unless alternative providers can be found. It is important to note that the mechanism to retain followership here is retention of strong material bait.

In John 6, after the multitudes had been miraculously fed with bread and fish, they followed Jesus to the other side of Lake Tiberias. When they asked Him at what time he got there, Jesus told them the truth that they wanted to be with Him because He had fed them, not because they understood the miraculous signs. He warned them not to be concerned about perishable things like food. He asked them to spend their energy seeking the eternal life that the Son of Man could give.

I would like to challenge you now in your relationship. Is it built on material needs? Ask yourself what would happen if you could provide those needs for yourself, would you still be in that relationship? If you would quit, then let us get out now and start spending our time seeking the eternal life that is based on nothing else but the truth. That our partners are buying us things and taking us out on expensive excursions is not the main reason to determine the worthiness to follow and stay with them. Let us ask ourselves this question; "if time brings disability and incapacity to this person will we stay with them unto death?" We must learn to use things and provide for ourselves not misuse people to achieve what we want.

People follow because of fear

Some people follow a leader because they are scared of what may happen to them if they don't. In my country during my days as a herd boy, I used to see others drag and savagely beat up their dogs when the dogs refused to follow them and go along to the pasturelands with them. The dogs would be dragged on a strap, crying out as they got into a tug-of-war with their leaders. I did not know then that there are similar forms of human leadership where people are forced to follow or else pay the price.

This form of leadership may be experienced in families where the spouse and children are dragged along against their will or in organizations where service delivery and achievements are placed ahead of the well-being of the people. The situation becomes worse in politics where some leaders compel statesmen to abide by their terms or else face brutal treatment that often is accompanied by massacres of the innocent citizens. There are many political leaders down through history have exuded this form of leadership. Idi Amin and Chaka Zulu are two good examples of this kind of leadership.

In this scenario, people are actually not led but driven from behind. It is a matter of life and death. Those who escape the unfortunate incidence of death are left with lifetime scars to prove it. The South

African apartheid system and other human revolutions demonstrate this sad reality. It often happens that there will be a day when enough will be enough. Then the tables turn and yield bitter fruits for the leader. This can be witnessed in the lives of Idi Amin the Ugandan, Chaka Zulu, and others of their kind in history.

Idi Amin was a member of the small Kakwa ethnic group in north-western Uganda. He was only slightly educated. In 1946, he secured a post as an assistant cook in the British colonial army known as the King's African Rifles. His swift rise through the ranks saw him serving in the Allied forces' Burma campaign in Myanmar during World War II and in the British action against the Mau Mau revolt of 1952–1956 in Kenya.

Amin was one of a few select Ugandan soldiers promoted to officer rank before the Ugandan independence in 1962, and he became intimately acquainted with Milton Obote, the new nation's prime minister and president. In 1966–1970 he was made chief of the army and air force. Following a difference with Obote, Amin organized and staged a successful military coup on 25 January 1971. He then installed himself as president and chief of the armed forces. In 1975 he became field marshal, followed immediately by becoming president for life in 1976.

Amin ruled directly, delegating very little power. He was well known for his unexpected changes of temper, from clowning to shrewdness and from kindness to totalitarianism. He frequently exuded extreme xenophobia. This was confirmed by his act to rid Uganda of all Asians in 1972 and his verbal berating of Great Britain and the United States as well as other world leaders. He was personally involved in the Palestinian hijacking of a French airliner to Entebbe in July 1976. He escalated tribalism to an extreme by allegedly ordering the persecution of Acholi, Lango, and other ethnic groups. Amin's brutality earned him a new title: he became known as the

"Butcher of Uganda." It is a general belief that during his presidential tenure over 300,000 people were murdered, while an innumerable multitude were tormented.

In October 1978 Amin ordered and launched an attack on Tanzania. With the aid of some Ugandan separatists, in the long run the Ugandan army was overrun by the Tanzanian troops. On 13 April 1979, with the Tanzanian-led forces closing in on Uganda's capital, Kampala, Amin fled the city. He escaped first to Libya before finally settling in Saudi Arabia.

Chaka was the son of Senzangakona, chieftain of the Zulu, and Nandi, an orphaned princess of the neighbouring Langeni clan. Since Senzangakona and Nandi belonged to the same clan, their marriage was a violation of the Zulu tradition, and as a result their child automatically bore the dishonour. When he reached the age of six, Chaka's parents separated, with Nandi taking her son back to the Langeni, where he passed a fatherless boyhood surrounded by individuals who detested his mother. In 1802 Nandi was driven out by the Langeni so that she finally took refuge with the Dletsheni, a subclan of the powerful Mtetwa. When Chaka was twenty-three, his Dletsheni age group was called up for military service by the Mtetwa paramount chieftain, Dingiswayo. For the next six years, he fiercely served as a warrior and darling of the Mtetwa territory.

Following the death of Senzangakona in 1816, Dingiswayo relieved Chaka of his army service and sent him to take over the Zulu, which at that time probably numbered no more than 1,500. They occupied an area on the White Umfolozi River in northern Kwazulu-Natal in South Africa. They were among the smallest of the more than 800 Eastern Nguni–Bantu clans. However, their journey to greatness commenced from the day of Chaka's arrival. Chaka ruled with an iron hand from the outset: his policy of intolerance to the slightest opposition was enforced by the death penalty.

Regarding the dogs that did not want to follow herders to the pastures: when the straps by which they were dragged broke, the dogs would run for their life, crying until they arrived home with their tails between their legs. That is characteristic of leadership where people do not follow eagerly. Every time the oppressed are looking for and devising ways to break free from their oppressors. Here the mechanism to keep followership is to maintain strong weaponry (i.e., use a strong leash or cage), and the bad words of the leader are equated to brutal orders and actions. The leader becomes a temporary winner. In politics this model has generated thousands of hunger and disease struck refugees.

People follow willingly for love of their leader.

This is the healthiest of leadership relations. Although the followers here see the leader as standing for everything they need, they make their own choice to follow, and their love keeps them behind the leader, in whom they see invaluable qualities. Such leaders put the interests and well-being of the people at the forefront, and followers feel their warmth and see their efforts on behalf of their followers' development. It is this form of leadership that may make the world a wonderful place for everyone to live in. The mechanism to keep followership here is being a humble servant, and the good words of the leader are matched by a reciprocal focussed action and determination backed by unfaltering discipline and integrity. Long after death this leadership yields positive results, and organizations keep growing.

That is why in 1 Peter 5: 1–4 (TEV), Peter appeals through Silvanus to the leaders of the church to be shepherds of the Lord's flock and to take care of it willingly, as He would like them to. He urges the leaders to do their work not for mere pay, but from a real desire to serve. He asks them not to try and rule over those who have been put in their care, but to be examples to the flock. He makes them a promise that when the Chief Shepherd appears, they will receive the glorious crown whose brilliance will never fade.

Peter makes it unmistakably clear that true leadership is never about self-reward. True leaders become humble servants of those they lead and even to flocks which do not belong to their fold so that they may find shade and shelter. The tendency in politics is to abandon those who do not belong to our organizations, forgetting that they are an important part of our nations.

Church leaders should also remember that those who are not members of our congregations are still children of our heavenly Father. We may differ in our ways to praise, but the spirit is one, and the same Father in heaven is praised. The same Creator has made us look at things differently so that we may complement each other in our weaknesses. If the whole world saw through one eye, it would die instantly, for it would be blind to a lot of things. That is the reason why even in nature there is genetic variation, to allow adaptation and continuity of species. Living organisms do not all fall under the plant or animal kingdoms, and even within the different kingdoms, there exists a myriad of different species.

REASONS WHY PEOPLE MAY WANT TO LEAD

Desire for Money

Generally, the higher one goes in leadership, the position is associated with more money and other benefits. This is where most of us as leaders fail to understand that we have to serve our followers. The rewards associated with the positions we occupy easily become our sole purpose in leading. When followers realize what is happening, their complaints often bring turbulence to our organizations. The driving force here is that such leaders want to accumulate as much money as possible, and unfortunately it is never quite enough. They then develop a strong desire to occupy the seats forever.

Desire for Power

Everybody wants greatness in some way or another. It is reasonable to enjoy being a great person in society as long as one serves the needs of that society. However, people often end up making others their slaves and thinking that all the best things should belong to them as bosses. Men quite naturally start thinking that even all the beautiful women should belong to their harem. This behaviour is analogous to the territorial behaviour displayed by various animals in the wild where the winner takes all. The tendency is to try and rule forever while killing those who might be perceived as threats.

Love for Others

There are those who are driven by sheer principles of love. These are true leaders, who see an opportunity to bring change for their people. Such leaders are fully aware of the challenges of leadership that may even lead to their death. Nevertheless, their love for others takes precedence. It often happens in this scenario that those who embark on the leadership journey do not consider family as their immediate relatives through blood ties; rather, anybody who adheres to the principles to achieve their goals is family. The driving force is the achievement of the good for all. That is why our Lord Jesus once said His brothers and sisters are those who obey the laws and teachings of His Father in heaven.

TRUE LEADERSHIP:

Take note, oh dear Theophilus, that in the year six (6) BC, a leader of leaders was born in a manger at Bethlehem in Judaea. He came to set practical standards on leadership. Every aspect of leadership taught by any of the so-called "leadership gurus" may be viewed as a subset to His all-encompassing model. His love for humankind made Him descend to become a servant of servants. He came as a result of a promise that was made to our father Adam—that the Lord would come to save him and his posterity after five and a half days according to the Book of Adam.

According to the Book of the Cave, the Lord's star appeared to the Magi two years before He was born. They saw the star in space which was brighter than any other star. Within the star was a maiden carrying a child, with a crown set upon his head. It was customary to the ancient kings, and the Magi of the Chaldeans, to consult the "signs of the Zodiac" concerning their affairs of life. The star brought unrest in the whole land of Persia. The kings, the Magi, and the wise men of Persia were stupefied and extremely afraid of the sign which they saw.

They subsequently thought that the king of the Greeks was determined to wage war against the land of Nimrod. They then consulted their books of wisdom, through which they understood and learned the truth. The Magi of the Chaldeans discovered that by means of the motions of the stars, among which they named the signs of the Zodiac, they were able to know and understand the significance of events before they took place. When the Magi read the "Revelation of Nimrod," they discovered therein that a king was born in Judah, and the whole path of the dispensation of the Lord was revealed unto them.

It is important to note that the star signalling the birth of the Messiah was not like the normal stars. It was brighter and could be seen in daylight. Hence this star was so bright that even the sun's light could mask it. This indeed confirms Jesus' words later when He said that He is the light of the world. Anyone who follows Him will have the light of life and will therefore never again walk in the dark. Note, oh dear Theophilus, that those who want to lead must be the light of the world. They must light the way and be exemplary unto those they lead. They must do this through maintaining the right attitude, self-control, and integrity, remaining true to the course to which they are called while keeping their eyes wide open to what is happening around them, so that they may lend a helping hand to others.

As leaders in our countries, communities, and various organizations, we must measure our actions in light of our responsibilities. Do our deeds provide light for others to follow? Or are we dragging those we lead to support our hidden agenda? Note that it is very hard to walk in darkness, where there are no clearly defined goals, mandate, or empowerment. In Matthew 5: 15–16, Jesus teaches that no one should light a lamp and put it under a bowl; instead, it should be put on a stand where it may provide light for everyone in the house. In the same way our light should shine before our people through the good things we do in integrity and discipline, so that our heavenly Father may be praised! We should be ambassadors of the kingdom of light.

According to the knowledge received from the longstanding tradition which had been passed down to them by their fathers, the Magi left the East and went up to the mountains of Nôdh, which lie inside the entrances to the east from the lands that border the north, and they took from them gold and myrrh and frankincense. According to the Book of the Cave, the Magi knew the whole service of the dispensation of our Redeemer, judging by the offerings they brought: the gold was for a king, the myrrh for a physician, and the frankincense for a priest. The Magi knew who He was and that He was a king, a physician, and a priest. It is said (Book of the Cave) that when the son of the king of Sheba was a little boy, his father had taken him to a rabbi where he had learned the Book of the Hebrews surpassing all his peers and countrymen, so that he explained to all his slaves that it was written in all the books of genealogy that the king would be born in Bethlehem.

When the Magi had made their preparations and were ready to go up, the kingdom of the mighty men of war was nervous and petrified. The Magi were followed by such a multitude that all the cities of the East, including Jerusalem, were shocked. When they came before Herod, he was awestruck and shaken, and he commanded them, saying that they should proceed in peace and carefully search for the young Child. Then, when they had found Him, they were to come and tell Herod where He was so that he too could go and pay his respects. However, Herod knew that his heart was devious. His reverence was only lip service. He was playing an innocent flower, and yet he was a serpent under it.

At the time when the Magi went up to Jerusalem, a great turmoil was stirred in Judea, due to the decree by Augustus Caesar, which demanded that every man was to be registered in his country and in the city of his fathers. To most leaders of the world, whenever we think or realize that a leader is arising who might command more power than we do, we become jealous and restless and sometimes even plot to kill the rising star. This behaviour is common even at an everyday workplace. This is why those who are well seasoned in leadership always preach that a leader must breed other leaders without regard to whether they will surpass him.

Note that the legacy of good leaders may not die even long after they have departed from the earth. Efforts to try and suppress their leadership result in the veneration and exaltation of their course. We should take an example from John the Baptist. When he saw Jesus coming to where he was baptizing, he said, "There is the Lamb of God, who takes away the sin of the world! This is the one I was talking about when I said, 'A man is coming after me, but he is greater than I am, because he existed before I was born.' I did not know who he would be, but I came baptizing with water in order to make him known to the people of Israel" (John 1: 29–31, TEV). Note that John was a leader, but he prepared the way for the one who was going to lead after him and be greater than he was.

When the Magi had gone forth from Jerusalem and from Herod's presence, the star which had been their guide on the road appeared to them, and they were delighted. The star went on before them until they entered the cave, where they saw the young Child wrapped in bands and laid in a manger. Along their way there they had said to one another, "When we arrive there, we shall see mighty and wonderful things, according to the law and custom which prevail among royal personages when a king is born." They thought that they would find in the land of Israel a royal palace, couches of gold with cushions laid upon them, the king and his son arrayed in purple, awestruck soldiers and companies of royal troops, the nobles of the kingdom paying him honour by presenting gifts, tables laid out with meats fit for the king, vessels of drink standing in rows, and men and women servants serving in fear. Such were the things which the Magi expected to see.

Instead, they saw sights far better than these when they went into the cave. They saw Joseph sitting in astonishment and Mary in a state of wonderment, but there was no sign of the furnishings and preparations which accompany royal state. Although they saw all this humility and poverty, they had no doubt in their minds, but they approached in fear and made obeisance to Him in honour, and they offered unto Him gold, myrrh, and frankincense. Mary and Joseph were aggrieved that they had nothing to set before the Magi, but the Magi ate their own provisions.

The world has developed its own set of standards by which it judges people. To be respected or be held in high esteem, one must look a certain way, own and display recognized material property, or occupy an important position. The Magi had a spiritual gift. Although they had expected to see certain things, they continued to make their obeisance to the Lord of lords even though he was born in material poverty. They approached in fear and respect and had no doubt in their minds. These are the people who do not judge the book by its cover, but know that the test of the pudding is in its taste.

Many of us have made choices in life based on how much people talk or how presentable they look, only to realize later that they are not what we thought them to be. I might now ask many people, "Is your partner what you initially thought of them? Is that employee what they presented at an interview?" Even most of the politicians have turned away from their campaign messages. They travel in expensive entourages, sounding sirens to drive aside the hungry commoners who installed them into power!

Whatever people may later turn out to be, we must treat them with respect and make them feel special even when they have revealed their true colours. In John 5: 5–6, we meet a man who had been bedridden for thirty-eight years. According to Sacret texts, his name was Longinus, and he was a Roman soldier. This is the man whom Jesus commanded to pick up his mat and walk—although we learn that on the way to the cross during Jesus' last days, this is the same man who spit in His face, slapped Him, and pierced His side! During his healing, Jesus had asked Longinus whether he wanted to get well. After the man was well, Jesus found him in the Temple and said, "Listen, you are well now; so stop sinning or something worse may happen to you" (vs. 14, TEV).

Recall the story of King Saul and David. When Saul saw that David was becoming famous, he was consumed by jealousy and wanted to kill him. But David had no ill intentions, and he spared Saul's life on two occasions when he could have taken advantage and killed him. In the first instance Saul was on a hunt for David and came to a cave where David and his men were hiding. Saul went into the cave to relieve himself. David saw him, crept over and cut a piece off Saul's robe without Saul knowing it (1 Samuel 24: 2–4). In the second instance, David and his men came to Saul's camp at Mount Hachilah. They found Saul and his men asleep, with Saul's spear stuck in the ground near his head. Instead of killing Saul, David commanded that they should take Saul's spear and water jar (1 Samuel 26: 11–12). David merely wanted to show Saul that he was not after his position in any way. He was satisfied that he would come to rule Israel at an appropriate and appointed time. The importance of relevant experience in leadership cannot be overemphasized. David knew this, and he was no position monger. Those who are well conversant with the challenges of leadership are not eager to lead—and when their time inexorably comes, they make good leaders. It is much different in the political sphere, where we often get confused managers ravenous for positions.

In Matthew 5: 43–48, Jesus teaches about love for enemies. He tells us to do well to those who hate us, bless those who curse us, and pray for those who ill treat us. If anyone hits us on one cheek, we should let them hit the other one too; if they take our coat, we should let them have our shirt as well. When someone asks for what belongs to us, we should not ask for it back. If we love only those who love us and do well to those who do the same to us, then there is no reward—for even the sinners do that! A spiritual reward comes when we do something out of the ordinary and challenge our faith. If as leaders of the world we would take this teaching and practice it, there would be absolutely no need to manufacture dangerous weapons meant for mass slaughter! The enemies we eliminate are no less human than ourselves.

Jesus said that no blind man may lead another one, for neither can see where they are going, and both may fall into a ditch. Without exception, all pupils learn from their teachers, and none of them is greater than their teacher. However, when their training is complete, every pupil will be like their teacher. From the foregoing, the importance of patience and listening may not be overemphasised.

Today most of the world is said to be ruled by democracy, but there is turmoil all over the continents. Is it hunger that has generated so much selfishness in us as leaders? Most governments are headed by family and friends to enjoy statutory benefits, while the ordinary citizens wail and if lucky survive off the scraps at the bottom of the food chain. Do we see clearly as leaders? How can we help take the speck out of our brothers' eyes while we sit with logs in our own eyes? When will we wake up as leaders to the fact that it is not by making difficult laws while enriching ourselves with material things that we may become good leaders? Instead it is through truly becoming humble servants to humanity! It is definitely not through proclamation of laws and orders meant to anchor our positions. Who can truly anchor their position when the next second they may be presented with death? No matter how rich one may be, people's true success in life is not measured by what they own! True success is defined by the percentage achieved on an individual's god-send mission through the journey of life.

That is why in Luke 12: 13–21 Jesus told the parable of a man who wanted to tear down his barns to build new bigger ones where he would store his corn and other goods. The man said to himself, "Lucky man! You have all the good things you need for many years. Take life easy, eat, drink, and enjoy yourself!" But the Lord said to him, "You fool! This very night you will have to give up your life; then who will get all these things you have kept for yourself?" Then this important question arises: How do we perceive and use our riches?

In leadership, knowing and caring about people is more important than endless technical knowhow. The hungry and the needy do not care how much you know until they know how much you care and that you demonstrate true effort to attend to their problems. What threatened the learned scribes and teachers of the law about Jesus was that His followers were quickly growing in numbers. It happened because He was a problem solver, a healer, and a friend. Above all, He had good skills with people. He knew how to handle people of different calibres. He was food to the hungry and water to the thirsty. He was a friend and a shepherd to those He led then, and He still is to us today, while He will remain thus to future generations!

True leaders should really be happy when they see future leaders emerging from their organizations. They should be willing to train and groom them so that their followers may in time surpass them. We must realize that, if our organizations are doing well during our leadership, they have to grow and do better with those who lead after us! If new leadership does not surpass our own, then organizations become stagnant and may lose membership and fall! There is room for growth only when succeeding leaders become better and better than their predecessors.

Predecessors lay foundations, while successors build on the foundations. However, to train and groom, one must have an eye to see who has potential to become a future leader. For it is a futile exercise to pump resources onto a nonresponsive candidate. If one is inert, our efforts to change them will do nothing if they are not willing to change. Nevertheless, the tendency in organizations is to suppress up-and-coming leaders and safeguard our positions. If only we understood that credit and praises are all due to the Father, the Son, and the Holy Spirit.

Recall the story of the prophet Elijah and Elisha, son of Shaphat, from Abel Meholah. Elijah groomed Elisha, and the day Elijah was to leave Elisha, taken by a whirlwind to heaven, Elijah thrice urged Elisha to remain behind but Elisha refused and said, "I swear by my loyalty to the living Lord and to you that I will not leave you"

(2 Kings 2: 6). Then at the end Elijah invited Elisha to request what he wanted before Elijah was taken away from him. Elisha asked for a double share of Elijah's power so that he could be his successor.

The important thing is that, although Elisha was groomed, he also wanted to lead, and he saw the importance of leading through the work and miracles that his master Elijah had performed. Elisha was oriented and inspired towards growth. That was why he did not just ask to become like his master, but he asked to be twice what his master had been. When Elijah went to heaven, he had performed seven miracles. However, Elisha doubled the number of miracles and performed fourteen. The last of Elisha's miracles was performed when people threw a corpse into his tomb and ran off. As soon as the dead body came into contact with Elisha's bones, the man came back to life and stood up.

John the Baptist exclaimed, "There is the Lamb of God, who takes away the sin of the world! This is the one I was talking about when I said, 'A man is coming after me, but he is greater than I am'" (John 1: 29–30). Although Jesus was greater than John in the kingdom of heaven, there is a very important hidden message in what John said. He told the people that he baptized with water while the one coming after him would baptize with fire and the Holy Spirit.

When John said Jesus was greater than he was, he also was referring to Jesus' mission. Although they were both sent by the Father, Jesus would go an extra mile to baptize with fire and the Holy Spirit. While John liberated with water, Jesus would liberate with His own blood! It does not mean that John was less gifted, but he was sent with a special mission which indeed he truly fulfilled. Jesus was to start from where all those messengers who came before Him on the same course had arrived and to better their work. Thus in leadership we should know our role and execute it well. Like a baton, power should be passed on smoothly from one leader to another.

An important lesson we should learn in leadership is that it is a process that does not come spontaneously. It is a process that requires input from the trainer and positive response from the trainee. In chemistry, I learned that in reaction conditions, the factors influencing the rate of reactions include temperature, agitation, pressure, and the presence of a catalyst. There must be contact between the molecules for them to react. Nonetheless, there are inert molecules which will not react regardless of any effort. It should be noted that there are also molecules with high affinity for others, and they react fast. In every reaction the most important thing would be the inputs and products formed. The question is whether the equilibrium shifts in such a way that the resultant is a high percentage of the desired products. In cellular organic reactions, the conditions that influence the equilibrium and the resulting products would be important for natural selection.

Temperature

When molecules are heated, they are energized and become entropic. At this stage they have a lot of potential energy to react. Likewise, in our lives we need to be heated to the right state in order for us to react, yield products, and succeed. We may be energized through mentorship, education, seed funding, or some other means, including some compliments when we do well. Once we have acquired the right potential energy, we are ready to react with other partners and yield results. We should not rule out adversity as an important agent of positive change!

Agitation

Shaking helps to create mobility and collisions that are important for reactions to start. You will definitely agree with me that those who are looking for something must move out of their so-called comfort zone. Those who are looking for jobs should market themselves by crafting résumés and applying. They must also make an effort to meet with the right people and be at the right places at the right time to state their case.

Those who want to find a marriage partner should act no differently. They should look after themselves very well and go out to meet people. This is where they may be seen, and someone may be attracted to them. Surely there is no way that anything can happen if they stay behind closed doors.

Life is very dynamic. There are also times when we may think we have done the best we could, but the question is, does our best suffice to trigger a positive reaction? In other words, is our best enough to reach the required threshold of reaction? The reason why there are Olympic winners and losers is because winners go an extra mile beyond the required threshold to get results!

Pressure

When the volume of a reaction vessel is kept constant and pressure is increased, this helps to bring molecules together and increase the chances they will collide and react. Adversity brings pressure into our lives and forces us to act in ways that we would not have under so-called normal circumstances. There are people who have been changed to become assets in their societies due to painful encounters such as jail, death of a loved one, and torment by stepparents; and some great discoveries and leaders have been born out of hopeless distress. I am not saying that we should be cruel to our fellow humans, but I am merely stating what pressure has done to people. At university I have seen students who were pushed by pressure to perform well.

Catalyst

Catalysts are known to speed up rates of reactions and direct the way an equilibrium should proceed. A catalyst works by binding reactants and bringing them together to react. Catalysts are important in our lives to make things happen. There are people who have the ability to create positive relationships and bring others together. In these meetings, partnerships and actions are begun that otherwise could not have happened. Sometimes such meetings give birth to great companies and unlock enormous potential. In teams, there are those players who act as catalysts. Their dribbling and passing facilitates scoring by others and therefore winning of games. Catalysts are very important in any organization.

In true leadership a leader puts the welfare of his followers first and trains and empowers other leaders. He does the odd jobs and he is prepared to die for his people instead of them dying while he enjoys life and protection. He guards his followers like a chicken brooding over its chickens instead of going around with an entourage of guards. His world revolves around the wellbeing of the people and not his position, and therefore everyone he meets is important. He is concerned about losing every single one of his followers. That is why he/she leaves the multitudes and becomes troubled about a single unwell individual.

In John 10: 11–13, Jesus says that he is a good shepherd who is willing to die for the sheep. He explains that when a hired man who is not a good shepherd or owner of the sheep sees a wolf coming, he abandons the sheep and runs away. Then the wolf seizes the sheep and scatters them. Have we ever asked ourselves as leaders whether we are willing to bear difficulties on behalf of those we lead or even die for them if it comes to that?—and if not, that we are just using them to fill our pockets with money or exploit them somehow for the sake of our fame? It is common to see leaders of the world with convoys and sirens. In some situations I have seen common drivers forced onto the sidewalk and damaging their vehicles against obstacles while giving way to the vehicles of so-called very important people (VIPs). Do not think I am suggesting that you should not give respect where it is due, but I am simply alarmed at the way the world approaches things. Why do we idolize ourselves so much when we do not show the slightest reverence for our Creator?

In democracy, "the rule of the people by the people for the people," I have seen leaders elected into office who, after being sworn into office, have become greater than those who elected them into power. Which brings me to ask, What is true power? I would define true power as the strength to control the feelings and desires of one's heart. Power is not instilling fear in others by virtue of holding an important position, owning material goods, owning a harem of women or having multiple love affairs. Let us be warned that these lures are deceptive, like mist that seems to cover the whole landscape to those who are within it, and yet it might extend for only a few kilometres before disappearing in the heat of the sun.

Remember, the greatest amongst us are those who are like children. In John 13, Jesus washes His disciples' feet. Peter does not understand how his Master could wash his feet. Jesus explains that if Peter does not want to be washed, then he can no longer be His disciple. After washing their feet Jesus asks them whether they understand what that means. He instructs them that He as their Master and Teacher has washed their feet; and so they must do the same to each other. He goes on to tell them that slaves are not greater than their masters and that messengers are never greater than those who sent them.

He set an example that, although we should be respected as leaders, we should serve others and do the odd jobs! Each one of us should be a bearer of the message from our heavenly Father and acknowledge that we are not acting on our own behalf. He demonstrated that leadership is about service, not positions.

In Matthew 20, after the mother of the sons of Zebedee had asked Jesus to promise her that her sons would sit on His right and left when

He became King, Jesus told her that she did not know what she was asking for. Jesus then asked the sons whether they could drink from the cup of suffering that He was about to drink. They answered that they could, and He told them that they would indeed drink from His cup. He told them that He did not have a right to choose who would sit on His right and left, for those places belong to those for whom His Father has prepared them.

The other disciples became very angry with the two brothers when they heard. Jesus called them all together and said, "You know that the rulers of the heathen have power over them, and the leaders have complete authority. This, however, is not the way it shall be among you. If one of you wants to be great, he must be a servant of the rest; and if one of you wants to be first, he must be the slave of the others—like the Son of Man, who did not come to be served, but to serve and to give His life to redeem many people" (Matthew 20: 25–28).

From this scripture, we learn that the sons of Zebedee and their mother did not know that they were prophesying about what would happen when Jesus would be crucified, that there would be two sinners—one on the right and the other on the left. The sons did not realize that heavenly leadership comes at a heavy price. The other ten disciples thought that the brothers were going to be given leadership positions. Jesus knew what they were thinking. He called them and explained to them that whoever wants to be great amongst others should be a servant to them. It is common that people aspire to high positions and to be greater than others, but we unfortunately do not understand that leaders are those who serve and do not see themselves as greater than anyone!

Jesus did not just educate His disciples to serve, but He gave them authority to do what He was doing. He wanted to make sure that the mission did not die down after His departure from the world. In

Matthew 10, Jesus called all His disciples and gave them authority to drive out evil spirits and to heal every disease and sickness. However, after He had sent them out and they returned with a report on what had happened, He told them the parable of the sower. He wanted them to know how people behave, since He was grooming them as future leaders who would be dealing with different characters. It is important to note that because Jesus has trained (and is still training) many leaders, who in turn train more leaders; His mission spreads to fill the whole world.

One other important aspect to true leadership is building good teams. As followership grows, it is important to build good teams of leaders who can help in division of labour and train others to perpetuate the goals of an organization. Jesus built His team of twelve, empowered them to do what He was doing, and charged them to pass the work on to others. That is why Christianity has prospered so much throughout the world. Building good teams has tremendous effects on organizational growth.

In Acts 2: 43–47, the Good News Bible says that numerous miracles and wonders were being done through the apostles, and believers continued to live together in close fellowship and shared their belongings with one another. They would sell their property and possessions, and according to the agreement they had set for themselves, they distributed the money among all, according to their individual requirements. Day after day they met as a group in the Temple, and they had their meals together as brethren in their homes, eating with glad and humble hearts, praising the Lord, and enjoying the good will of all the people. And daily the Lord did not stop adding to their number those who were converted and saved.

It is important to note that the miracles and wonders were being done through the apostles, not by the apostles. Without the power and grace of the one who had sent them, the apostles could not do anything. They were tools of the one who groomed and sent them. For their Master had once told them that no student is superior to his teacher and that slaves are never greater than their masters. The apostles' obedience and respect for their Master, made it easy for the Master to perform great miracles and wonders through them.

We are also told that the apostles were joined as a strong team that took care of the needs of each other without selfishness. Note that selfishness destroys teams, and there is no way any team with selfish players may win cups! Even in praising and serving the Lord, He is made glad by our joint effort. Hence, there is more soul harvesting when believers, pastors, and churches stop bad-mouthing and fighting against one another and instead reinforce each other's efforts. A kingdom divided amongst itself is a waste! Even in our families, the acts of infidelity born out of lust lead to family destruction and impaired achievements. Innocent children end up as victims.

Sharing within a team is important as it cements the team together. That is why Christian marriages are solemnised in community of property. This is for team building. When we share things, we learn to be humble and shed property hoarding. We learn to say, "It is ours," not "It is mine" and to take good care of things for the benefit of others. Team members eat together and do a lot together; they are a family and they grow used to and complete each other instead of competing against each other. Then our Father in heaven adds a lot to our joint efforts where we complete instead of competing against our teammates. When we look at the natural resources of the world (air, water, minerals, biodiversity, etc.), we see that the Creator has made them in such a way that we must jointly use them for the benefit of everybody, including future generations.

Today there have arisen a number of issues that raise concern to the whole world: poverty, climate change and the environment, health, and some others. To successfully address these issues, the world must come together and be one big team through state and organizational leaders. For this to happen, we should look at the world as one body with many parts that should function well to achieve the goodness and well-being of the whole.

It is not strange therefore that in 1 Corinthians 12: 12–30, the apostle Paul wrote that Christ is like a single body, which has got various parts. Even though it is made up of different parts, it is still one body. He went on to clarify that in similar manner, all the nations of the world; whether they be Jews or Gentiles, whether they be subjects or masters, have all been baptized into the same single body of the Spirit. We have all been given the one Spirit to drink, for the body is made up of many parts instead of one. If the foot were to claim that it does not belong to the body because it is not a hand, surely that would not exempt it from being a part of the body. If the ear would claim not to belong to the body for the mere fact that it is not an eye, that would not excuse it from being a part of the body either. If the whole body were just an eye, hearing would not be possible. If the whole body were an ear, smelling would be impossible. The Creator has resourcefully put every different part in the body just as He wanted it to be. The body would not exist in its present form if it were all only one part.

As in the world there are different continents, and in the continents there are different countries, America may not say, "I don't need you, Africa." Africa may not say, "I don't need Asia." In Africa and in America, all the nations that live there also need each other, as do the provinces in any one country. The same thing applies to Muslims and Christians, Roman Catholics and Pentecostals. We exist because the One who has created the whole universe has allowed us to exist for a purpose. No one is better than the other.

The most important response for us is to acknowledge the love of our Father in heaven and each live as our Father requires. We have heard in the Law that "we must not murder," "we must not commit adultery," "we must love and honour our Lord," "we must love our neighbours," "we must not steal," and "we must do unto others as we would like them to do unto us." We have all been given the same terms of reference whether we are African, Asian, American, European, Muslim or Christian, President or subject, educated or illiterate, rich or poor, old or young, and mad or "normal."

So then, how can the eye claim that it does not need the hand? Nor the head assert that it does not need the feet? It is a blatant truth that we cannot do without the parts of the body that seem to be pathetic. Contrarily, the body parts that we think are not worthy are the ones we give the greater attention. The parts of the body which do not look very lovely are taken care of with special modesty that is not needed for the more beautiful parts. Hence there is no division in the body, but all its various parts have the same concern for each other. Should any part of the body suffer, all the other parts suffer with it; if one part is honoured; all the other parts share its delight.

As humans are we less effective and less sensible than a swarm of bees? For a swarm of bees understands there is a king and queen, workers and soldiers. All the parts in a swarm play their role effectively so that there can be honey! In leadership we have to understand and perform our roles well for our teams to achieve intended goals. In a pack of African spotted wild dogs, the policy is that "no one eats unless we all eat."

Remember then, brothers and sisters, that the greatest among leaders and our teams is the one who serves others! There may be different talents and gifts amongst us, but the greatest of those are the ones that benefit the whole. Hence, the apostle Paul wrote in 1 Corinthians 12: 4–11, that spiritual gifts exist in many different kinds, but they are given by the same Spirit. There are numerous ways of serving as there are many peoples of the world, but there is one Lord to be served. The service may be performed in different degrees of ability, but the same Father gives capacity to all His people for their specific service. The Spirit's presence is expressed in some particular way in each individual for the benefit of all. The Spirit gives one person a message full of wisdom, while to another person the same Spirit gives a message full of knowledge. However, it is one and the same Spirit who performs all these according to His wish and plans. He offers a different gift to each person.

In a game of soccer, if a player dribbles and displays his skills on the ball without letting his teammates interact so that he becomes part of a flowing game, then he is only causing confusion. Likewise, if a person speaks in strange spiritual tongues so that the whole congregation does not understand, he or she is only causing confusion, for no one can hear and be saved. But those who proclaim the message in clear language are doing great service to others, and they are likely to spiritually heal others and bring in converts to the church. In the whole church, the different gifts, if used orderly, together achieve the good of the whole church.

From the foregoing, be aware, oh dear Theophilus, that with leadership come challenges, some of which may lead to death. There are people who are so absorbed and determined in their evil ways that they will set themselves against the message of the truth by all means.

In John 8: 43–45, Jesus asked the Jews why they could not understand what He was saying. He argued it was because they could not bear to listen to His message. He called them the children of their father, the devil, and proclaimed that they wanted to follow their father's wishes. He explained that from the very beginning the devil was a killer and has never been on the side of the truth, because none exists in him. When the devil tells a lie, he is only acting out what is natural to him, because he is a liar and the instigator of all lies.

One of the pillars of true leadership is remaining faithful to the truth no matter what the circumstances may be. Remember, integrity is such an important character to any leader, and without the truth there is no integrity. If the world rejects you because of the truth, recall that the world is full of thieves and robbers; but the good shepherd lays his life for the sheep. Remember, the message of truth comes not from you but from Him who sent you! Jesus said that, like Him, we are the light of the world, and we should act thus. Hence, like Him we came not to judge the world but to save it. Then to lead we must build up our strength in union with the Lord and by means of His mighty power.

The apostle Paul in Ephesians 6: 11–20, urges us to put on all the armour that the Lord gives us, so that we may be able to stand up against the devil's evil tricks. We should be aware that we are not fighting against human beings but against the wicked spiritual forces in the heavenly world, the rulers, authorities, and cosmic powers of this dark age. So let us put on the armour of the Lord now! Then when the evil day comes, we will be able to resist the enemy's attacks, and after fighting to the end, we will still hold our ground.

We should stand ready, with the truth as a belt tight round our waists, with righteousness as our breastplate, and for our shoes the readiness to announce the Good News of harmony. At all times we should carry faith as a shield, for with it we are able to put out all the burning arrows shot by the evil one. Salvation we should accept as a helmet and the Word of the Lord as the sword which the Spirit gives us.

All these we must pursue in prayer, asking for the Lord's help, and we must pray on every occasion, led by the Holy Spirit. We must keep a watchful eye and never give up, praying always for all of the Lord's people. Paul concludes by asking that his followers should pray also for him, that the Lord would give him a message when he is ready to speak, so that he could speak boldly and reveal the secret of the gospel. For the sake of the gospel he was an ambassador, even though he was in prison. He asked them to pray that he could be bold in speaking about the gospel as he had to.

The armour of the Lord is made up of the truth, righteousness, the Good News of peace, faith, salvation, and His Word. The apostle said that the truth should be tight round our waists. This is crucially important for leadership, because anyone whose waist is unfastened easily becomes a victim in the acts of lust and fornication. Whether a man or woman, if they are engaged in adultery, those who follow them lose respect and trust in them—unless of course they lead other adulterers. The truth as a belt is also an important centrepiece because all the other parts of the armour will wobble loosely if not tied neatly together, impeding our ability to fight properly.

Righteousness refers to decency, morality, honesty, and justice. A leader who does not observe morality, honesty and justice is caught up in deeds that degenerate his or her character, and those who follow lose their trust unless they are of the same character, in which case they may not be able to see any value discrepancy. If righteousness is our breastplate, then we are not easily pierced by the arrows of the opponent, who wants to disintegrate us with his lies. It is righteousness that helps us see all people as equal and treat them with due respect and fairness without prejudice.

Our leadership should be anchored by the Good News of peace. Whether we are kings, presidents, or organizational leaders, if we do not have the Good News of peace to help us build and share with those we lead, then our associations are short-lived, for no one would like to be in the company of a rude, disrespectful leader where coarse language is the order of the day. Where there is a message of peace, people are free to voice their views and act willingly without pressure. If the Good News of peace be our shoes, then we hold fast and stand firm on the ground during any kind of conflict. We should be ready to announce the Good News of peace as our form of defence against the evil one.

Faith is important because without it, we may not be able to move an inch towards our goals. Every organization has goals to work towards. Because the goals define a future state which is only conceptualized in our minds, it is very important to maintain good faith in order to achieve them. Without faith our minds work against us, and we fail even before we start working towards our objectives. The law of life is the law of belief, and without faith we may not believe.

A helmet of salvation guards our heads so that they may not be chopped off. If salvation is our helmet, it means that the Lord Himself is our helmet, since Jesus' name means "The Lord is salvation." Hence, the helmet is His blood through which we were bought. Remember that in the journey our doorposts were daubed in the blood of the lamb so that the angel of death would be able to pass over and spare our lives. If the blood of Jesus is our helmet, then death may not destroy us! During the day of destruction we will be spared, for our foreheads will glimmer with the blood of the Saviour.

When one leads a team into any war, all members need to be sure they have organized sound defensive mechanisms before launching their attack. Whether it is a platoon of soldiers or a soccer or basketball team, without proper defence they are bound to lose. It is like walking into war without armour. We may easily be killed. That is why we may only march into war with our spiritual spear once we have our armour on. We may lead our teams into the wars of life once they are armoured with the right skills. In the journey we saw how important it was for Moses to acquire and be armoured with the right skills before marching with the army of the Israelites into a barren wilderness where he could easily endanger all their lives.

We should do all things praying and asking the Lord for help. If He does not go ahead of us in anything we do, then we risk failing, for we may not see ahead of us. That is why Israel could not move or break camp unless the pillar of cloud or fire moved. If we refer back to the diagram on time, only the Lord and those vested with part of His visionary powers may be able to see what is to confront us ahead. Breaking camp at our own time depending on our desires may lead us into serious trouble, self-destruction, and even death. The mercy and love of our heavenly Father towards every one of us is immeasurable! Hence, that is why it is so important to move at His appointed time and pace.

Mercy is a very important virtue of a good leader. Merciful leaders are not ruthless to their followers, and they may not keep on pushing towards their goals and desires without considering what it will do to others. With mercy goes the power to forgive—a rare quality of the brave! It was demonstrated by Nelson Mandela and Moshoeshoe the first, founder and ruler of the Basotho nation.

As Moshoeshoe and his people migrated from his former fortress in Botha Bothe to Thaba-Bosiu, cannibals caught and ate his grandfather. When the cannibals were caught, he asked that they be given food and not be killed, as was the general will of the majority. In South Africa, many selfless iconic leaders rose to fight apartheid, a cruel, ungodly racial discrimination rule against non-white South Africans. Nelson Mandela was one who rose to fight for freedom against all odds. The conditions of the day made his life and those of his comrades a nightmare! Following twenty-seven years of imprisonment, he became the first black South African president. Instead of taking revenge on his torturers, he came up with the "peace and reconciliation policy."

These and others are men and women who have immortalised themselves in deeds. Their actions possess no stench of selfishness.

They did not care whether their lives would be lost to gain peace, happiness, and freedom for their fellow humans. Their portraits will be displayed in history's memory vaults for ages to come.

Throughout Jesus' mission, we discover this important nature. Through mercy He helped the gentiles who were otherwise considered as dogs under the Law. He rescued the woman caught in adultery and healed the blind. He put the wellness of the people before the Law, for the Law sometimes puts heavy burdens on people without helping to solve their problems. A good leader weighs the situation and makes the right decision. It is amazing that on the cross at Calvary, our Redeemer asked the Father in heaven to forgive His murderers, for they did not know what they were doing.

As Christ is our leader as Christians, we have to strive to follow His examples. He lived and still lives according to His preaching. If we had mercy, there would be no raping of defenceless children, mothers, and grandmothers. The cries of those begging for our mercy would crack our stony hearts! It is mercy that would let hijackers and raiders spare innocent lives. The same mercy would give our conscience scruples against lying about our brothers and sisters so that they end up in jail for crimes they did not commit! It is mercy that stops us from destroying other people's families through lust, for our conscience tells us to worry about what they and their children will go through! With mercy we do not eat in the sight of the hungry as if nothing is wrong! If we each could have mercy on others now, our Father in heaven would do the same for us and make the world a better place! Hallelujah!

Good leadership does not breed revenge. In Matthew 5: 38–39 Jesus said, "You have heard that it was said, 'An eye for an eye, and a tooth for a tooth.' But now I tell you: do not take revenge on someone who wrongs you. If anyone slaps you on the right cheek, let him slap your left cheek too." Truly, I tell you today, without the aid of our Father in heaven, no one does any of these things! We are quick to fight back wherever we can. When not satisfied with something, instead of praying about the situation, we take to the streets or look for quick vindictive measures.

Today it is common practice for many of us to do things to be recognised and praised by the world. Good leaders never do things to be praised by the world! Their focus is on true liberation of those they lead, and they know their reward is in the spiritual world! Their true pay comes from the world beyond, the world flowing with milk and honey, the world in and around paradise! In Matthew 6: 1–4 Jesus says, "Make sure you do not perform your religious duties in public so that people will see what you do. If you do these things publicly, you will not have any reward from your Father in heaven … Then it will be a private matter. And your Father, who sees what you do in private, will reward you."

As politicians and as church and organizational leaders, are the things we do they meant exclusively for our fame and personal gain? Then we might have innocently failed dismally, for our reward may not come forth from the heavenly Father. Sometimes we may make such claims as that we are doing acts of charity and giving to the needy. If the primary reason we are doing these things is to promote ourselves and not the Father, then they are futile actions and rob us of our eternal reward! We should not love ourselves more than we love our Father in heaven, for too much love for self leads to selfishness which breeds all forms of corruption. Remember, the great commandment is "Love and honour your Father in heaven with all your heart and soul" and secondly, "Love thy neighbour, and do unto others as you would like to be done unto you." If you want to lead, love and obey the Lord and those He has put in leadership positions. Then you may be loved and obeyed by others when it is your turn to lead! Love, mercy, serving, submission, humility, and integrity are important for leadership. Of these, I would like us to discuss love in the next chapter.

It is important to note that I am not referring to position leaders here. For position leaders it is very hard to groom anyone who is not a close member of their families or a close friend. That is why today we see many political leaders clinging onto their seats, preferring to die there rather than hand the position over to others. I would like to refer to the example of Moses, who despite being told that he would not cross the Jordan to the Promised Land, made a smooth handover to Joshua, the son of Nun, whom he had groomed.

Moses was a great leader! However, during his last days, his journey culminated with climbing the rocky mass of Mount Nebo. It was only upon reaching the summit that his eyes saw the wonderful sight of the Promised Land, the land he and the Israelites had tried to reach for forty arduous years. To him what mattered was that the younger generation of Israel would finally enjoy the promise made to their grandfathers. He was not selfish like some of us who would like to enrich ourselves and not partake in anything if it does not bring us immediate returns.

The same applies to our Redeemer: during His last days he climbed a mountain with a burden of our sins in spirit and the cross to wear him physically. Instead of focussing on himself, he prayed to His Father to take care of those He had chosen, those who were not of the world. He was referring to His followers so that they could be given strength. When they cried for Him on the cross at Calvary, He told them to cry instead for themselves and for their children. This kind of behaviour is not common except for those who are in the Father, and the Father is in them! Hence, those anointed of the Lord have clear knowledge of where they are going!

The apostle Paul groomed Timothy and gave him this instruction when he was in prison:

> As for you, my son, be strong through the grace that is ours in union with Christ Jesus. Take the teachings that you heard me proclaim in the presence of many witnesses, and entrust them to reliable people, who will be able to teach others also.
>
> Take your part in suffering, as a loyal soldier of Christ Jesus. A soldier on active service wants to please his commanding officer and so does not get mixed up in the affairs of civilian life. An athlete who runs in the race cannot win the price unless he obeys the rules. (2 Tim. 2: 1–5 TEV)

Hence the most important thing that Paul wanted to impart to Timothy was continuity of leadership which should come through grooming and empowering others to perpetuate the message. There are important rules for the leadership to continue. Timothy had to understand that it is characterized by teaching others, good conduct, knowing one's purpose in life; steadfast faith, patience, endurance, persecutions, sufferings, mercy, and love.

Jesus says that His Father has given Him all things. He says that the Son is known to no one except the Father, and likewise the Father is known to no one except the Son and those to whom the Son decides to reveal Him. He calls all of us who are tired of hauling heavy loads to come to Him so that He may in turn give us rest. He urges us to take His yoke and put it on us and to learn from Him, because He is temperate and meek in spirit; and He assures us that we will find rest. He promises to put an easy yoke and light load on us (Matt. 11: 27–30).

Therefore, my brethren, it is only fair to conclude this chapter by a tribute to one of the most outstanding and exemplary leaders of our time. He is an easy example because our world can easily identify him since he has recently wrought amazing deeds in our midst.

Tribute to President Nelson Rolihlahla Mandela

The world is in deep agony for they have lost a grandfather, a father, a husband, a brother, a companion and friend. However, the reality is that you have changed form and continue to live forever. Your arduous autobiography is etched onto the subconscious minds of men—where a portrait of your long walk to freedom dangles not to gather dust. Indeed you have preserved yourself in your deeds. What you have become to humankind will not be obliterated from history.

You lived your life as a humble servant to humanity. You have taught the world that true leadership is not about self-veneration and prominence above others, for there is one in heaven to whom these things eternally belong. You have taken the most difficult parts of the Scripture and made them practical: "love thy neighbour, do unto others as you would like done unto you, forgive others that you may be forgiven, let children come to me for the kingdom of heaven is theirs, love your enemies." It is amazing how multitudes fail dismally to practice these excerpts, even ministers of the Word, but to you they rolled out naturally like a long-practiced piece of performance art!

My heart knocks against the bars of my rib cage and threatens to tear the pericardium as it wants to peep through to the outer world. I sincerely begin to understand the pain you went through for twenty-seven years as you yearned to connect with your beloved and the world! You were subjected to mixed emotions that were meant to gradually erode your strength to oblivion. From the moment you set your foot in jail, you grew from strength to strength as the negligible building blocks of time slowly constructed the twenty-seven onerous years. The certainty of the future could only be determined through a seasoned subconscious mind, fixing one's eyes on celestial forces. You and we are today separated by the flailing curtain that separates heaven and earth. Our language is different, for now you speak that of heavenly beings and the angels—*tecel cat marith macha* ("Let us all praise Him").

Through spiritual eyes I look beyond the river of mortal life. I see a tall, handsome man briskly striding towards the golden gates in the city of the Lamb. I call desperately but he does not steal a backward glance, for he is beckoned by saints of old and the heavenly troops unto whom his attention is entirely focussed. In his ears the echo of my voice fades to nothingness with the swift increments of the distance between us. Whither he rushes a banquet is prepared for him, and his Master will give him a pat on the shoulder and say, "Well done, son!" He is marked by the scars impressed as he drudged though the thorny scrubs to liberate his people in the desert of apartheid. The soles of his feet are sore from sand bleach; his tongue sticks to the palate due to thirst and hunger for love, peace, and harmony in the world. His face is scorched by the blazing sun, but internal life and peace exude through the radiance of his flickering eyes and a genuine smile.

The undulating hills of Mveso have become amoebic – as like amoeba they have formed projections in preparation to engulf your organic remains and slowly digest and set them free to join the cycles of nature. You remain a wonder to the world. Had you been a landscape, you would have unanimously made it to the world heritage list! The place where your remains are buried is therefore an important heritage site! Goodbye, *Tata!* I feel this is the only way I may deal with the catastrophe of your loss and the avalanche of emotions evoked by your exodus! You have united people in your life and departure. To that, testimony is given by the multitudes around the world who speak in one voice, and those who gathered around your Houghton home to sing as they delivered their flowers and condolences from dawn to dusk. Let your legacy be entrenched in all nations throughout generations to come!

Madiba, on 27 April 1994 you cast your first vote to turn a sod towards your nation's democracy. You breathed a sigh of freedom and relief. Your ballot paper was like an invaluable cheque that purchased a piece of land upon which all countrymen and comrades may live in love, harmony and peace. This momentous event unravelled through the pages in your subconscious, and brought to the fore of your cognitive mind the reality of a cross-section through the population of the heroes and heroines of your soil whose blood watered the seed of your country's germinating democracy! These are men and women who slipped in the frozen glacial political landscape of apartheid to donate the irrevocable and priceless gift of their lives. Indeed as you have rightly said in your words, the sun shall never set on so glorious a human achievement!

We thank the positive forces—the organization and people alike who nurtured your political birth and development. They trained you and gave you a stage on which to perform. Combined with your willingness and resilience against the blistering sun and adverse weather of the time, you germinated and developed to bear the fruits we enjoy today. You and others carried your nation through difficult times. Your knees did not buckle under the burgeoning load of racial discrimination and dehumanization instituted by the prevailing conditions in your environs. Instead you soldiered on, prepared to meet any circumstance nature threw your way—*Hamba kahle Mkhondo!*

To the whole world and friends, let us loose the man and let him go. To the flowers that grow in our hinterland, the sweet-smelling flowers transplanted from the sweltering eastern shores of our seas and from the glimmering slopes and glades of our countryside to contribute in the beautification of the landscapes of Qunu, we are deeply thankful for rendering his farewell dignified and colourful. It would be total unfairness not to express benthic gratitude to those who worked to audaciously organise such a dignified sending away for our father! Long live Madiba! Goodbye, Tata! You have raised the leadership bar to be perched upon by the most majestic of birds—the bearded vulture (*Gypaetus barbatus meridionalis*) iconic and common to our high jagged mountains.

Love

Chapter 5

There is a powerful force that transcends even the most fortified barriers, whether they are natural or man-made. Walls with moats have been traversed whenever the force commands. Through the barricade of spears and guns, love has infiltrated. It has sneaked through the rib cages to restore wrecked hearts and to demolish even the strongest hearts so that they stoop and submissively plead for mercy. Love like a mortar has cemented relationships and helped them grow into grand walls, but it has also dwindled to bring huge structures to ruin.

Like an aircraft, love has flown over distances and ferried people over continents. Those on board have settled in air and unfastened their seat belts. Miles above the ground they are intermittently treated to delicacies and move around to ease their muscles. However, there are times of turbulence when everyone is shaken with anxiety. Turbulences vary in magnitude and duration. Some force the plane to come down after the flight crew have given a bracing command. If any, the survivors of the ordeal and their next of kin sustain irrevocable scars.

As a ship, love has borne multitudes across seas. Those not taking the trip have often stood on pier bridges and brandished their goodbyes as the machine cuts open the water blanket ahead. Far in the deep ocean sometimes icebergs and storms arise. The ship becomes tempest-tossed, inducing trepidation in those on board. The worst-case scenario terminates with the wreckage and sinking of the ship. A myriad of dangers seal the fate of those who were on board.

Likewise a tourist train leaves a station with scores of tourists. It makes its way through a beautiful countryside. Passengers are from time to time doped with a dose of environmental scenes. They peep through the windows and admire as the kestrel suspends its flight in air and flaps its wings above the green undulating grassland sporadically marked by rocky hills with tufts of the broom karee (*Rhus erosa*). They soon come to forested gorges where serrated cliffs rise and fall into wonderfully carved masses of landscape. Then without warning the train derails and plunges down the steep mountainside. The surroundings reverberate with the wails that mask the hiss of the rivers and melodies of the birds.

Love is the cool spring that quenches your thirst when you are parched and drained. It is also a furious river that engulfs, hurls, and vomits you dead onto its banks to be devoured by scavengers as it constantly flows and hisses miles downstream. It is an acid that causes heartburn and an emulsion that soothes it. It is a gentle wind that fans our faces in the heat of the sizzling sun, and a storm that alters and lays waste the landscape. It is food that nourishes the body to a beautiful round figure—and venom that siphons the bodily fluids so that we are left scrawny skeletons.

Love is the medium of support that makes us soar to great heights and summit the insurmountable peaks. It is also the means though which we glide and descend to the deepest dungeons of life. In love we have an anchor that keeps our vessels affixed on the shoreline as the waves rise and fall. However, over time it shakes the shore loose, threatening even the lives of innocent bystanders. It is a dagger by which we smite our enemies but one by which we may also fall, as it was a case with ancient Roman soldiers under tremendous pressure of war.

The flowers of love are varied in colour and morphology. Their assortment looks wonderful on the countryside, but to some their pollen grains are a cause of sneezing and allergy. From them the bees collect nectar to create sweet aromatic honey. Although it is so sweet and enticing, honey gatherers should be extra careful and safeguard themselves against bee stings. A brim-full cup of hot chocolate is dangerous not only to those enjoying it if it spills over. Those in the vicinity may have their garments stained, or they may too sustain burns.

It is love that has clothed us and hid our disfigured bodies from the laughter and scorn of our enemies. Yet it is love that has ripped our garments and stripped us so that our foes may momentarily mock and take glory in our plight. Oh, love! What a wonderful thing! The lovely beginning promises a good end; the journey of love takes a burden off the travellers; the laws of love twist the hand of the heart seeking its obeisance, while those who lead with love are swarmed by cheerful followers, and the law of love is the law of life: it is greater than all, and it keeps the universe united.

Love is a complex subject. It is widely talked about, written of, and sung about. However, love is rarely practised. It is not common in the world we live in; otherwise our world would be paradise! We may not easily realize as we keep talking about love that it is not easy to practise. Various types of love have been defined, but one important thing I have realized is that love is painful to practise. To be able to love, we must be prepared to shed our selfish desires, and to do this we undergo pain, for it is not easy to deprive our flesh of its needs. The apostle Paul has written thus of love:

> Meanwhile these three remain: faith, hope, and love; and the greatest of these is love. Love is patient and kind; it is not jealous or conceited or proud; love is not ill-mannered or selfish or irritable; love does not

keep a record of wrongs; love is not happy with evil,
but is happy with the truth. Love never gives up; and
its faith, hope, and patience never fail. Love is eternal.
(1 Cor. 13: 13, 4–8, TEV)

When we have no faith in someone, it means that we have no trust or confidence in them. However, hope on the other hand means expecting, anticipating, wishing, or looking forward to something. To love means to adore, worship, or to be devoted to something. In other words it is difficult to have true love for someone we do not have faith and hope in. I would like us to break down what Paul wrote as follows:

Love is patient and kind

Love is hard to wear down, and its endurance is timeless. Clearly we are not referring to circumstantial relationships in which conditions dictate the course of action and the outcome. These are parasitic associations between people where personal gains are a driving force spelling out the life of a relationship. How strong such relationships are depends on the strength of the needs that bind such people together. When I studied chemistry, I learned of weak hydrogen bonds between atoms and stronger electronic bonds that may vary from single to double and triple bonds. Hydrogen bonds are a loose association and require little excitation energy to break. In organic chemistry, a single bond breaks faster than a double bond, which breaks faster than a triple bond when energised. Likewise, human beings exhibit relationships of varying strength—the strongest being those governed by unconditional love.

In a weak relationship, there is no patience. Any small entropy results in breakdown, for there is only a very weak bond uniting those who are in that relationship together. When such affairs fall apart, it is almost like nothing has happened. However, other relationships are bound by and are subject to stronger bonds. They need a lot of activation energy to break the bonds. When such affiliations dismantle, a lot becomes at stake.

Since true love is patient and kind, there is harmony in bonding and harmony without. That is why in true leadership we have seen that a good leader is happy with those who follow but knows that not all will embark on the journey. Those who do not want to take the journey are happily let go! Because our heavenly Father is patient and kind, He does not force His creation to worship Him. He wants us to worship out of good will. Hence, those who are sent from above let others follow them out of good will without oppression.

We are well aware of the story from the book of Ruth in the Bible where a woman named Naomi lost her husband and two sons, Chilion and Mahlon, in the land of Moab. After her two daughters-in-law had escorted her back to her land of Judah, Naomi asked them to go back to their homes and marry again, as she could no longer provide husbands for them. She told them that the Lord had turned against her and that she felt sorry for them. The daughters-in-law started crying, and Orpah kissed Naomi goodbye and went back home, but Ruth clung to her mother-in-law. Naomi told Ruth that her sister-in-law had gone back to her people and her god, and she also implored Ruth to go back like her.

Ruth replied that she should not ask her to leave. Ruth said, "Let me go with you. Wherever you go, I will go; wherever you live, I will live. Your people will be my people, and your God will be my God. Wherever you die, I will die, and that is where I will be buried. May the Lord's worst punishment come upon me if I let anything but death separate me from you!" (Ruth 1: 16–17, TEV).

There are times when our love is tested. It is not that Orpah did not love her mother-in-law, but the type of bond they had shared could not stand the test of time. It could not stand unbreakable, as the activation energy was far beyond its threshold of integrity. Ruth's endurance and readiness to give up everything to stay with her mother-in-law is uncommon and unconditional love. The bond she shared with her mother-in-law could not be shaken by circumstances. Naomi's love for her daughters-in-law was free and not compelling. She wanted them to stay with her by their own choice, not under coercion. Hence, when Naomi saw that Ruth was determined to stay with her, she could not say anything more.

When Naomi and Ruth arrived in Bethlehem, everybody there got excited that Naomi was back. When the women called her by the name Naomi, she asked them to call her Marah, for she was convinced that her Creator had made her life bitter. She explained that she had left Judah with plenty, but the Lord had brought her back without a thing. She wanted to be called Marah (bitter) instead of Naomi (pleasant), for in her eyes the Lord had condemned her and sent her trouble.

In times of trouble, the world becomes like a jungle where only the fittest may survive. Many friendships and social affiliations break down, leading to everyone seeking their way out. We often forget that even after the worst of storms there will be a warm and sunny day. In the aftermath, the land shall rehabilitate. If our spiritual eyes remain fixed on the heavenly things, there is no need to change our names during times of trouble. Otherwise we would have many names, since time throws a myriad of events to deal with during one's lifetime. We are still the person that the Lord created, even though we may be under duress today and be happy tomorrow. The truth is that we have to undergo the necessary moulding in order to enter the next stage in our life. It is not easy to shed the past and enter into an unknown future! It is endurance and hope that make possible our next success. In the book of Job, the Lord blessed the second part of Job's life even more than He had blessed the first.

When Naomi and Ruth arrived in Bethlehem, it was the onset of the barley harvest. Naomi had a relative named Boaz from the family of her husband Elimelech. One day Ruth asked her mother-in-law if she might go and glean in the fields behind the harvest workers. With her permission, Ruth went to the fields and walked behind the workers, picking up what they left behind. The Lord guided her to be in the field that belonged to Boaz. When Boaz arrived in the field and asked the man in charge who Ruth was, it was explained that Ruth was the woman who came with Naomi from the land of Moab. She had been toiling since early morning and had just taken a short rest under a shelter.

When you think that you have lost all, when Elimelech, Chilion, and Mahlon are gone, and you are left without a husband or son, the Lord knows you have been working hard, and He will send a Boaz who will be kind to you. It is true that you have been toiling from morning to night, seven days, a month, a year, or longer; but now it is time to take a break under the shelter of the Lord. You will drink from the water jars you have not filled. You will enjoy the kindness of love from a quarter you do not expect. Remember, all things belong to the Lord, and He uses them at His appointed time on whomever He wishes. The Lord has surely seen and heard about all the things you have done for others. Now it is payback time, time for the Lord to reward you for the enduring love and kindness you have shown to Him through others. It is time for you to have bread and dip it in the sauce when you least expect it. Naomi never knew where her meals would come from, let alone the thought of having a grandson. However, not only did the Lord provide for her meals, but He gave her an important grandson in the genealogy of the Jews. It might have only been then that Naomi and Ruth began to understand why they had to go through all the trying times.

When I lost my job at the beginning of 2010, I thought it would only take a short time to secure another one. After all, I had qualifications and good experience. I had connections with important people who gave me assurances, especially in view of my curriculum vitae (CV). They all pointed to the strength of my CV, but to my surprise years rolled without my getting a job, even those jobs I had applied for where I perfectly qualified. Men and women who knew me from school (my classmates and those I have taught) and those with whom I have worked in different jobs did not understand why I went such a long time without a job.

During this time I tried different avenues but to no avail. I prayed hard with frustration for the Lord to make possible some breaks and even thought that He had abandoned me. What made matters worse was the loss of my two daughters and a close friend in a tragic car accident in the midst of joblessness and poverty. However, I later discovered that every situation that I thought was a good opportunity could have actually landed me in trouble. I then could see how much the Lord had loved me for not making those opportunities realizable. Our Father's plans are different from what we think. What we see as a good opportunity may not look the same to Him. When He gives at His appointed time, the world remains shocked beyond words! My experiences, although painful, have turned into an invaluable heavenly lecture and have made me realize that His love for people is patient, kind, and immeasurable!

Love is not jealous or conceited or proud

Jealousy and pride are born out of selfishness as it is the core for all evil. Selfish people do not wish others well, and even though they own the best of anything, they are not satisfied. Pride is an enemy of humility and submission. Those full of pride will never repent, for they think doing so discredits them. They think that being apologetic is a sign of weakness. The reality is that pride is a sin that has led Satan out of paradise, and likewise those full of pride are his disciples and are not worthy of a place in the City of the Lamb.

Although King David displayed selfishness and greed by taking Uriah the Hittite's wife (2 Sam. 11), his lack of pride made it easy for him to submit and repent when the prophet Nathan reprimanded him. David had been rescued from Saul and had been given Saul's wives. He had been made ruler over Israel and Judah. As if all that was not enough, he desired and wanted to own the only important thing Uriah had. It is very common that we may be given a lot of things but never stop desiring our brothers' houses and possessions. My spiritual father and mentor has often exhorted me to be content with what I have. Many leaders through history have killed and confiscated property from the weak. What makes matters worse is that they are proud following their covetous deeds. What helped David was his true remorse when the prophet opened his eyes to the sin he had committed (2 Sam. 12: 7).

In the book of Esther, she invites the king and Haman to a banquet (Esther 5: 7–6: 13). After the banquet Haman was jubilant, but his happiness was turned to fury by the fact that Mordecai the Jew who was sitting at the entrance of the palace did not rise or show any sign of respect to him. On getting home, Haman invited his friends and asked his wife Zeresh to join in. He boasted to them about his richness and that he was more important than any of the king's officials for Queen Esther had given a banquet to him and the king and nobody else. He reiterated that they were invited back the following day. However, he mentioned that none of what he told them meant a thing as long as Mordecai sat at the entrance of the palace. Haman's wife and friends suggested that he build a gallows twenty-two metres tall on which he could ask the king to hang Mordecai the next morning.

It so happened that that same night the king could not get to sleep. He ordered that all the official records of the empire be read to him. By divine power, part of what they read included how Mordecai had exposed the plan by Bigthana and Teresh to assassinate the king.

Then it came to the king that Mordecai had not been honoured for saving his life. When the king asked whether any of his officials were in the palace, the servants answered that Haman was there to see the king (he had come to ask the king to hang Mordecai). When Haman was in the palace, the king requested his counsel for honouring an important man.

Since Haman thought that the king wanted to honour him, he asked the king to order that his royal robes be brought for the man. He went on to ask the king to order a royal ornament to be put on the king's horse. Then one of the highest noblemen was to dress and lead the honoured man mounted on the king's horse through the city square. Then the nobleman was to announce these words, "See how the king rewards a person he wishes to honour!" Then the king ordered Haman to hurry and provide the honours to Mordecai.

After the service was performed, Mordecai went back to the palace entrance while Haman rushed home covering his face in shame. Matters got worse in the second banquet, when Queen Esther revealed to the king that Haman was a persecutor of the Jews and that he wanted to exterminate them. It also came to light that Haman had erected a gallows on which to hang Mordecai, the saver of the king's life. The king was very angry and ordered that Haman be hanged on the gallows he had prepared for Mordecai. Let us be content with what we have and always remember that the evil we desire for others, we instead desire for ourselves through the law of our own subconscious mind.

Love is not ill-mannered or selfish or irritable

Love is polite, for it respects and has high regard for others. When we have love, we understand that each one of us is a creature of the highest Creator, created to fulfil a definite purpose. When we look at one another, we must see our Father in each one of us! Satan has never created any human being and never will. At creation, the Bible says, God created man and breathed His Spirit into him. If the Spirit of God has been breathed into us, then we each have part of Him in us. Therefore, brethren, note that to be rude to one another is to be offensive to the Father!

As we have seen, selfishness is the root for all forms of evil—not money, as is often said. Those who care about themselves without regard for others will go to extreme lengths to get what they want. Whether they hurt or kill in the process does not matter. The most important goal to them is to fulfil the desires of their hearts.

Agrippina, the mother to Emperor Nero, instigated many murders in her house in order to fulfil her lust for the Roman Empire. Her actions led to a chain of evils, and her boy, who had earlier been a good boy, was transformed into a monster and a killer who ended up killing not only multitudes but also his own mother. The evil that we do unto others ends up coming back to us in the long run.

Love does not keep a record of wrongs

To be filled with love is to be free in spirit. The only way to attain this freedom is through forgiveness, which is a prerogative of the brave—and love is therefore brave! Bravery is more often mistaken for fighting and winning physical wars. In many cultures individuals are considered brave when they savagely fight and cause injury or even death to others. Our young boys grow up feeling that humility and calm are weaknesses associated with being less of a man. There are many in our societies who feel that forgiving and asking for forgiveness is equal to displaying weakness.

The secret is that when we forgive those who have wronged us, we are actually forgiving ourselves. It is said that we should not judge others so that we may not be judged. The same measure that we use for others will be used against us. We have to forgive our brothers from the depths of our hearts. In Matthew 18: 21–35, Jesus tells the parable of the unforgiving servant. Peter had asked how many times he had to forgive if his brother kept on sinning against him. Jesus told him that we have to forgive seventy times seven times, not seven times as Peter had asked.

Jesus went on to say that a certain king was going through his servants' accounts when one of those, who owed him millions of pounds, was brought in. Since this servant could not pay his debt, the king ordered that he be sold as a slave with all his family and all they had in order to settle the debt. This servant desperately pleaded for mercy and promised that he would pay back everything to the king. His king felt sorry for him and erased his debt.

When the man left the king, he came across his fellow servant who owed him some money. He attacked and choked his fellow servant, demanding his money back. The other servant begged for mercy in vain. His fellow servant threw him in jail until he could pay the debt. On seeing what had happened, the king's other servants went and reported the matter to the king. The king became furious and called the servant whom he had earlier forgiven. The king explained that this servant should have had mercy on his fellow servant as the king had had mercy on him. In his anger, the king sent this servant to jail for punishment until the whole amount he owed to the king could be paid.

Likewise we commit many sins against the Lord our Creator every day through many acts. The Lord forgives us, but oftentimes it becomes a fuss when we have to forgive our fellow human beings who have wronged us. Let us be aware that when we refuse to forgive others, our heavenly Father will also not forgive us. Thus we are holding back our own opportunity for freedom.

As love does not keep a record of wrongs, it does not keep a record of rights either! Many of us keep exhaustive lists of things that we may have done for others. In doing this, we fail to see that the Lord may use anyone to perform any good deed that He wants done for our fellow humans. A pawn that makes the last move to win the game of chess may not claim credit towards the win, for it has been moved by the player, and that move builds onto a number of moves that have been made by other pawns! Often we keep these lists to later intimidate or put others under our control, since they feel indebted to us for the good we may have done for them. In any good we do, our heavenly Father is the player making all the right moves, stirring us in this and that direction. Remember that when we keep a record of wrongs, we run the risk of our filter bursting as we have seen under the earlier discussion on time.

Fights spring up over what people think they have done for others. Some render help to others in times of need and later expect and make claims that their kindness should be paid back. True love does not expect to be loved back, for it is unconditional and expects nothing in return but the welfare of those loved. It is common to spend money and use materials on others to influence their love. Does it work? Only if alternatively better conditions may not arise that may lure them away. We have seen under leadership that if people follow under compulsion by circumstances, when they feel that their burdens are abated, they disengage. Acts of good deeds towards our fellow humans should not be in expectation for payback.

Today's world is characterised by scarcity of jobs. Many of our men and women have lost their dignity due to ignorance and lack of understanding. Our young women have forfeited their virginity at the hands of men who do not even love them. They are used to quench men's lust and dumped. In these relationships they think that their needs are supplied by their abusers. I call to you now, please know that your needs are supplied by your Father in heaven through your own mind.

Love is deeper and nobler than a mere exchange of gifts for sexual purposes. It is what we each feed to our minds that makes us who we are. Let us learn to be thankful for what we have. By being thankful, we come to be at peace with the universe and nature. It is in a state of peace and true love that our minds become creative. In this state we can engage in meditative prayer. If we stay in the heavenly love, we may ask for what we want, and it shall be done.

It is only if we ask that we may receive, only if we seek that we find, and the door is opened for those who knock. The critical questions are; are we asking for the right things the right way from the right source? Are we seeking the right things at the right time in the right place and manner? Are we knocking at the right door, at the right time, using the correct approach? Remember, as long as we stay in His love and keep His word, we are amply supplied.

Take heed, oh my dear beloved brother, that although we go around with elaborate lists of flaws from others' and our own past, the Lord is always ready to forgive and forget! This is the main reason why Jesus related the parable of the prodigal son (Luke 15: 11–32). Although the careless son had left and spent all his wealth recklessly on prostitutes in a distant land, the first place he remembered when he was in trouble and everything was going wrong was his home. He knew he had a loving father who would never forsake him. He knew his father's house would never run out of abundance. On returning to his father, the son was received with a welcome-home celebration. What are you waiting for? Go home to your Father! A feast will be prepared for you. It does not matter how tainted you think you are. Yes, you have committed sins, and you pass judgement on yourself and others. The reality is that God is love, and "love does not keep a record of wrongs."

In the gospel we are not told that the father questioned his son about his life in the distant land. We know the young man was looking after pigs, so his daily life must have been soiled with pig dung, and he must have smelled like pig droppings. However, as smelly and dirty as he appeared, the father was just happy to get his son back! (I may just presume that a hot bath and perfumed lotions/cream might have been prepared for him before he joined the table.) The most important thing is that a table laden with delicacies was prepared for him. His father never asked how his life with the pigs in the distant land was; he did not want to spoil the celebration and moment with trivial talk. His father's kingdom was a place of love where salvation was the central topic to feed to men's minds! There was no time to ask about pigs, as they were not welcome there. The conversation here was of divine things, not pigs! His brown teeth, chapped skin and bad breath did not matter to the father. Those could be dealt with later.

Every time we dwell on the past and relate horrors of the past, we impress wrong memories onto our subconscious minds and therefore hold on to the past—and such is the prominent characteristic of the media in our daily lives. "How was your life with the pigs? Why are your teeth so brown? Why did you decide to come back home? Oh, you look so pale! How do you feel now?" In the spiritual realm, what matters is the inner person. Whether the physical body is deformed or disproportionate by physical appearance according to human standards really does not matter! Our thoughts are the most important as indeed every one of us is the sum total of our daily thoughts! Therefore, it is important that we learn to watch our thinking pattern.

Love never gives up; and its faith, hope, and patience never fail

Faith and hope should be integral parts of our daily lives. Without patience, our faith and hope fade away, leading us to give up and fail in the end. Whether it is on business, social, and political relationships where we may want certain situations to change in our favour, we have to learn to be patient with faith and hope. The reason why many of us end up failing is because if no change is experienced on our expected time line, we think that our Father in heaven must be asleep, or perhaps we might have embarked on the wrong journey. Brethren, have we not learned that wine matures with age and that a thirty-year-old wine is not like a three-year-old one? Therefore old wine is tastier and more expensive to buy than new wine!

When I was a little boy, my grandmother used to relate to us fictitious but educational tales of long ago as we sat and listened intently to her around a flickering evening fire at the centre of a traditional round dwelling. One of these was a story of a prince who was engaged to a certain princess. The prince fell in love with a princess who would later become his wife. The first time he saw her from a distance, when his father had taken him along on a visit to the faraway land of their kingdom, his heart skipped with fright before he had even thought of proposing to her. They were both in their teen years by then. That same night when he went to sleep, he had a dream in which he heard a stranger telling him that the princess he had seen was his wife-to-be. The next day he was disturbed as if something had been planted in his heart. He did not know how to meet and talk to this girl. Eventually during the same year he visited her land, met her, and talked to her. It took time for her to fall in love with him. As a result of the genuine feeling that drove him, he waited patiently for her to say yes.

Eventually they agreed to take the matter to their parents and told them that they would like a marriage to be arranged between them. Their parents agreed, and the prince went on to pay a deposit for the bride price as was customary—although this was a small amount in today's terms. The plan was to arrange a big marriage ceremony, fit for royalty. However, during preparations things changed. Some gentleman came along who stole the princess's heart, and they eloped. Since they were both Christian members of their church, and the church did not allow marriages that were not solemnized in church through a wedding ceremony, they had to be separated so that a proper wedding could be arranged for them. It was during their short separation that the prince met the princess and asked her why she had rejected him to marry another man. She explained that she no longer felt love for him, and it would be almost impossible for her to spend the rest of her life with someone she no longer loved.

My grandmother would expressively relate that the prince was deeply hurt and did not see then how he would survive or get through the situation. After graduating from the traditional initiation programme, he arranged to leave his country to look for a job in a different country as part of self rehabilitation. This time he had momentarily lost interest in life on earth and had thought to himself that he would no longer have a relationship with any woman.

His former fiancée and the man who had snatched her from him were ultimately wedded. It was on the nightfall of the wedding day that the prince had a strange dream, and he explained it thus to his parents:

"I saw myself walking along a narrow path in green grassland in a land I did not know. My direction was heading east. I travelled until I came to where I entered through a gate to what looked like fenced grassland. The land was green and beautiful. Since I had walked for a long time, I was fatigued and thirsty. It is in this land where I saw a big rock under which came a spring of crystal-clear cold water. I knelt down and drank. Then I saw two male lions along my narrow path on either side. The lions were lying down facing each other, swaying their heads and opening their mouths in a yawn-like gesture. The narrow path led between them. It suddenly occurred to me that the lions could attack and kill me. In fear I crouched below the rock, attempting to hide. It was at this moment that a whirlwind shaped light descended upon the rock. From the light came a word that said, "Prince Sylvester, when things happen to you on earth, you think that God does not like you? Tell me, who is holding back these lions so that they do not kill and devour you?"

Grandma would demonstrate that in fear the prince woke up with his whole body wet, shivering and tired. He suddenly remembered that it was the wedding day. He prayed and loosed the princess and wished her well. Then my grandmother would ease herself, give a small grin, and explain that it is a common human error to think that we are God-forsaken whenever we go through rough patches in the journey of life. However, history bears evidence that all great men and women have been modelled and shaped by unforgiving circumstances. One of the laws of nature states that "for every action, there is an equal and opposite reaction." The forces exerted on us model us into echelons of glorious human achievement if we maintain a positive attitude. This we do through keeping our internal eyes on wonderful visions that signify peace, love, and freedom.

Some years later, during one of his holiday trips, the prince was walking along a warm sandy beach under a clear blue firmament in the afternoon sun when something strange happened. He met the princess, who was now married, taking a walk towards him on the beach. They both could not believe their eyes. They ran into each other's arms without thinking a second about it. Then they found a quiet, cool place to sit on some of the black rock outcrops along the shore. They discussed what had happened to each one of them ever since they had parted. As the thin gentle wind touched their faces, it unravelled the feelings that had never truly left the depths of their inner minds. Her marriage life was a living nightmare, since her husband was very abusive. Although she was now with a baby boy, they decided to move back together and take care of the child. They got married and lived happily ever after. Then Grandma would emphasise the importance of not giving up faith and then point out that it was time to go to bed—and, as if we did not know, remind us of the importance of tomorrow. "Love never gives up; and its faith, hope, and patience never fail."

There is no greater love that a person may have for his friends than to give his life for them. This is the love our Father and Redeemer from Nazareth gave for us. He came to cleanse our sins and teach us to love one another as He loves us. Love is the greatest law that governs the universe. When there is love, all is at peace and our heavenly Father makes us receive things that were meant for our prosperity in our lives. To love is to forgive and accept one another as worthy, just as the Father loves each one of us the way we are. It is important to be aware that His love to every one of us is eternal. We only get lost because we hate the Father and His Son and their message of salvation.

In John 15: 18, Jesus talks about the world's hatred. He says that we would not be guilty of sin if He had not come and revealed the truth about the Father to us (vs. 23–24). As it is today, we are guilty in many ways of sin for abusing the love that descended from heaven to wash away our sins. In John chapter 5, after healing a man by the pool, Jesus meets the man in the temple and tells him not to sin again so that something worse than his previous condition may not befall him. We would not be guilty of sin if the good news of love had never been preached to us. It is worse when ministers of the Word run off with other men's wives or get involved in ungodly deals after descending from the pulpit. It requires unconditional love to become a shepherd who enters the sheepfold by the gate and takes care of the weak. It requires us as men and women of the Word to understand that we are surrogate fathers and mothers.

> "When, Lord, did we ever see you hungry and feed
> you, or thirsty and give you a drink? When did we

see you a stranger and welcome you in our homes, or naked and clothe you? When did we ever see you sick or in prison, and visit you? ... I tell you, whatever you did this for one of the least important of these members of my family, you did for me!" (Matt. 25: 37–39, 40, TEV).

When our Lord prayed at Gethsemane for the Father to take the cup of suffering from Him, His soul was heavily laden with our sins. However, love for His Father and humanity made Him go through with the redemption plan. He recalled that no one from the heavenly creatures had wanted to come on earth when the Father had asked, "Whom shall I send?"

Although the evil one would want our Saviour to give up, as our father Adam had given in to temptation in the beginning, love prevailed for Jesus to go through with the plan. From Gethsemane all the way to Calvary, the devil wanted the Redeemer to give up, knowing that the death of the Redeemer was to set humanity free from bondage. The shame on Satan actually came when blood and water came forth from Jesus' side on the cross. Satan knew that this was the blood with which humanity would soak their doorposts and be set free from the wrath of God while the springs of life-giving water would change the structure and minds of people.

Take note, oh my brother Theophilus, that according to Sacret texts, Christ was born of Mary, the daughter of Jehoachin and Danah, who was betrothed to Joseph. He was born in Bethlehem of Judaea where He was laid in a manger, for the world provided no room for Him, for indeed He was not of the world. During his circumcision at eight days of age, He was carried by Simeon in the Temple of Solomon, rebuilt under Herod. He grew up in Galilee and must have learned His scriptures in the synagogue like all baby Jews of His time as per the Jewish custom. Towards the end of His journey to the cross He ate the Passover in the house of Nicodemus, the brother to Joseph of Râmethâ. He was bound in the house of Hannân, struck with a reed on the head in the house of Caiaphas, was bound to the pillar and scourged to faintness in the Praetorium of Pilate, the roman official, and on Friday the first day of Nîsân (April), the fourteenth day of the moon, our Redeemer suffered the weight of our sin.

It was during the first hour of Friday when our father Adam was created from dust. It should be noted that at the first hour of Friday, the descendants of Adam spat in the face of the Son of Man. While at the second hour of Friday all creatures gathered around Adam and bowed down before him as he gave them names, at the second hour the Jews gathered against the Son of God in fury and exclaimed, "Crucify Him!" Regarding the latter, David wrote in Psalm 22: 12–13 (TEV): "Many enemies surround me like bulls; they are all round me, like fierce bulls from the land of Bashan. They open their mouths like lions, roaring and tearing at me."

It is also important for us to take note that on the third hour of Friday our father Adam's head was clothed and beaming with the crown of glory. However, our Saviour was crowned with thorns during the third hour of Friday. For three hours Adam was in glory shining with majesty, and for three hours Christ was under judgement and trampled by Adam's descendants. Hence David wrote in Psalm 22: 6–7 (TEV), "But I am no longer a human being; I am a worm, despised and scorned by everyone! All who see me make fun of me; they stick out their tongues and shake their heads."

In the garden of Eden, it was at the sixth hour when Eve went up to the tree in the middle of the garden and saw how beautiful it was and how wonderful it would be to eat its fruit and become wise, contrary to the commandment of our Creator. So she indulged in the fruit of the tree. It was also at the sixth hour that Prince Emmanuel mounted the Cross, the tree of life, to set humanity free from iniquity. It was also at the sixth hour when Moses ascended the rocky mass and made it to the zenith of Mount Nebo to behold the wonders beyond the Jordan, the land flowing with milk and honey. At the sixth hour Adam received and ate the fruit of the gall of death from Eve, which the evil serpent had given her, while at the sixth hour Christ received vinegar and gall from those killing Him.

Take note, dear beloved of the Lord, that our father Adam spent three hours under the tree naked, and for three hours was the Saviour naked on the cross on Calvary. In the story of creation, we are told that the Creator made Adam fall asleep, and from his side he extracted material to create Eve. Hence, from the right side of Adam went forth Eve, the mother of mortal offspring and bondage. When the Son of Man hung on the cross, they pierced His side, and from His right side went forth water and blood. The water was for baptism, the mother of immortal offspring and eternal freedom.

It was on Friday when Adam and Eve sinned, and it was also on Friday when the earth was rent in a cross on Golgotha, and Adam and Eve received remittance of their sin and baptism. Hence, on Friday Adam and Eve died and were thrown out of paradise, and on Friday they were raised to eternal life through unfathomable love. They were freed from the authority of death that reigned over them. While they became naked on Friday, Jesus, the eternal Love, stripped Himself naked on the cross to clothe them and their offspring. Indeed the greatest love a person can have for his friends is to give his life for them! The door of paradise was shut for Adam and Eve on Friday; the Son opened it for them and their posterity on Friday, including the robber who was crucified with Him. On Friday the curtain hanging in the Temple was torn in two from top to bottom as priesthood, kingdom, and prophecy that had been bestowed to Adam were stripped off the Jews. At the ninth hour, Adam forfeited Paradise and went down into the lowest depth of the earth, and at the ninth hour the Prince of peace descended the wooden cross to the lowest depths of the earth, to those who lay in the dust. In His death, our Lord raised many to life, so that the prophecy that says one man should die so that many should be saved did come true. *"Eloi, Eloi, lama sabachthani?"* This is the extent to which selfless love goes!

Earlier the sons of Zebedee and their mother had asked Jesus to promise that they would be seated on His right and left when He became king. Jesus had told them that these places belong to those for whom the Father has prepared them. When He prayed at Gethsemane for the cup of suffering to be taken away, the sons of Zebedee and the other apostles could not stay awake, although they had claimed they could drink from the same cup. This was a mission well beyond their capacity. It was not as easy and straightforward as they would think. They never knew that even the heavenly beings had declined to drink from this cup of suffering. The majority of the disciples did not show their faces at Calvary! As Moses had walked with men and women but he climbed the rocky mass on Mount Nebo alone to behold the wonders of the Promised Land, Jesus was alone with sinners on the cross on Golgotha to behold the wonders of humankind's salvation.

No one can compare to the one who comes from above. Those who are the offspring of the earth belong to the earth and speak of things from the earth, but those who come from heaven are above everything, for even their knowledge is not of the earth. They preach and bear true witness of what they have seen and heard, yet no one accepts their message. However, whoever accepts their message confirms through their deeds that God is truthful. Those who are sent by God speak His words, because God gives them the comprehensiveness of His Spirit. The heavenly Father loves His Son and our Saviour so that He has placed everything of the kingdom of heaven in His power. Everybody who believes in the Son will have everlasting life. However, those who contravene the Son and His rules will not have life, but will suffer under punishment from the Father (John 3: 31–36).

Please take note, dear beloved of God, that in the spiritual world there is no time or space! For when events move at speeds approaching, equal to, or beyond c (the speed of light), time and distance approach zero (0). Hence everything will be laid bare in the spiritual world for everyone to see, from the beginning to the end of time! Let love and harmony not flee our midst. May the love of the Father, the Son, and the Holy Spirit be with you! Let prosperity, good health, peace, wisdom, forgiveness, respect, guidance, success, and everlasting joy be yours!

Conclusion

In the African wilderness, the matriarch elephant and her herd roam vast distances dictated by the seasonal changes in the landscape. Some in the group have just beheld glory through the arrival of a newborn. The strategy for protection against the elements breaks down as the daily survival pressure mounts. In the chaotic pandemonium of a siege by hungry lions, one of the newly born is exposed and killed. The journey is halted for some days as the herd mourn the tragic loss of one of their own in deep anguish. The pride and the cubs celebrate over what is to them a well-deserved meal.

In a distance the lioness has hidden her cubs from insatiable and harsh male lions which may attack and kill them. In their inquisitive and playful act, the cubs leave their concealed den. One wanders far beyond safety. He is attacked and injured by enemies. In his disorderly escape he goes over a muddy and slippery riverbank. In a frantic search, the mother lioness hears the desperate groans of her cub in the distance. She rushes over, hoping to rescue him. The mission fails dismally as the only thing she can do is watch her cub slowly slip into a fuming river. It is a painful goodbye as she reluctantly turns away with a sore heart on the verdict. The baby elephant is not even completely digested in her bowels.

In the open savannah the ostrich leaves her newly hatched chicks. In the heat of the sun pieces of quartz ignite fire by acting like convex lenses. Soon the frenzied blazes engulf the grass, turning it into an expanse of charcoal and ashes. The fire stimulates germination and diversity of some species. The ostrich comes running from a distant forage land. She is startled by what she discovers. What was at daybreak afro-combed silky-feathered beauty has been charred to crumbs beyond recognition. Her curdled frustration goes without consolation. Such is the daunting reality of life!

High on the branches of the willow trees, the spotted-backed weaver (*Ploceus cucullatus*) has ingeniously weaved his pendant nest. The neatness of the nest will give him advantages to mate and propagate his genetic legacy. Luckily the mate is impressed, and a courtship is sealed. A raging summer storm comes with gusty winds. The trees are badly shaken, branches break, and nests fall, scattering eggs into a messy scene. Breeding dreams are provisionally broken. However, the species will proliferate, and they never give up the quest!

The laws of creation/nature are fixed and may not change. All living things must adapt to suit the conditions and become resistant and successful. The laws of creation are the laws of life, love, and harmony. Humans introduce their own laws that contravene life, love, and harmony. The response of the universe is through disasters to those who try to amend its laws. Unfortunately, the mantle of gloom affects innocent bystanders too!

Whether we are African or American, European or Asian; we are part of the same creation. We share the same planet although occupying its different geographical regions. We each have adapted to our way of life through thousands of years of inheritance and improvement. Our phenotypes and genotypes are mechanisms that make survival possible in our different environments. These include the colour and type of skin, the colour, type and length of hair. There is part of us which is not depended on biophysical environment or ethnicity. This is the spirit, which is not confined by time or distance. It is not dependant on the colour of the skin, the hair or type of body within which it abides. It is certainly not subject to gender either. This is part of us which should dominate our perishable cage.

It therefore follows that despite where we may come from or live; despite our physical characteristics, appearance, and circumstances; we possess and should be ruled by the same spirit. The spirit which was breathed into our father Adam and Eve at creation. The spirit which is invisible and invincible for it is part of God. Then if God lives in us who and what can prevail against us? I visualise and hear a lot of questions and claims that, "there is a lot not going wright in our lives now, and how can you say that?" Indeed there is a lot but allow me to invite you to go treasure hunting with me in the *Glory of the sons of God*!

About the Author

Paul Maluke Nkofo was born on Sunday, 26 October 1969, at the village of Ha 'Matafita in Matebeng in the district of Qacha's Nek of the kingdom of Lesotho. He is the sixth child in the family of seven, comprising four girls and three boys. He was born and raised in poverty, where obtaining formal education was an enormous struggle.

Paul went through most of his primary education in Matebeng. In 1984 he moved to the district of Thaba-Tseka where he attended and completed his higher primary school with a first class. He then proceeded to do his junior secondary education which he completed, obtaining a merit certificate. Then he pursued a high school education to obtain a school living certificate in which he achieved a first class.

After high school, Paul and others were called to attend a six-month maths and science course, after which they registered for a bachelor of science degree at university level. Paul successfully completed and graduated with his biology and chemistry degree. His dream of studying the molecular biology of cancer was not realized due to circumstances beyond his control. He then settled for further studies in environmental microbiology in which he obtained his honours through coursework and research. Following his honours he enrolled for a two-year masters by research, working on water quality using molecular techniques.

On completion of his studies he lectured in biology at university level for three years. He worked and struggled as an entrepreneur, running his business in printing and graphic design, barely making enough to pay rent and to survive. Through grace, he later became part of environmental conservation projects as a district project officer, where he did extensive work building community awareness on environment and natural resource conservation, establishing conservation and sustainable use areas.

Paul got married at the age of thirty. He was blessed with four daughters. Of the four daughters, Mathabo Tabitha Nkofo and Mantšanana Beatrice Matsoso were involved in a tragic car collision on the afternoon of 4 June 2011, only five kilometres from home, where they died instantly with a close friend. The remaining two daughters are the eldest and the youngest.

In 2003 he lost his elder brother who was mysteriously shot; the case was never taken to trial. He then became part of bilateral conservation initiatives on natural and cultural heritage in trans-boundary regions. He took part in development of various conservation strategies in southern Africa. While working as one of the consultants in conservation management, he ended up as an overall coordinator on one of the multi-stakeholder projects.

When the projects ended, he vigorously looked for another job but could not secure any. He then decided to embark on his long-standing dream to write books. As an ordained preacher in one of the spiritually based churches of southern Africa, with a membership estimated at a hundred and fifty thousand, he thought it would make sense that his first manuscript should be on issues of faith in order to reach and appeal to a wide audience across the globe. Indeed he hopes that this humble manuscript may change the lives of millions across continents.